Thinking Thi

General Editors
Graham Slater and C. S. Rodd

6. The Sacraments

Thinking Things Through

Already Published

The Bible
C. S. Rodd

Worship
Michael J. Townsend

The Christian and People of Other Faiths
Peter D. Bishop

Why Evil and Suffering?
C. S. Rodd

Is There Life After Death?
C. S. Rodd

In Preparation

What To Do?
Richard G. Jones

Thinking Things Through

6. The Sacraments

Michael J. Townsend

EPWORTH PRESS

ISBN 0-7162-0524-6

First published 1999
by Epworth Press
20 Ivatt Way,
Peterborough
PE3 7PG

Typeset by C. S. Rodd
Printed and bound by
Biddles Ltd
Guildford and King's Lynn

Contents

General Introduction

The great Swiss theologian, Hans Küng, has said that his aim in all his writings is to enable his readers to hold their faith with confidence and not with a bad conscience. This new series, prompted by the conviction that Christians need to think through their faith but often lack appropriate help in so doing, has a similar aim. Moreover, the assistance that it seeks to offer is related to another conviction: that many church members need persuading that theologians are concerned in any way with their problems and that theology can be at all relevant to their lives.

In such a situation, it is essential, we are sure, to begin with life and with church life. Only in that way can we be confident that we are dealing with grassroots issues. Plainly, however, it is not enough to identify the questions where they arise; we must also indicate the sources of help – if not of all the answers – in as non-technical a way as possible.

In some volumes, these tasks will be tackled in sequence; in others, they will be interwoven. Whatever the precise format, however, our hope is that, through this interaction, difficulties will be faced, fears dispelled, open discussion promoted, and faith informed and strengthened.

The books can either be read by individuals on their own or used in groups. We hope the questions at the end of each chapter will be useful both as a check that the text has been understood and as a spur to reflection and discussion.

Later volumes will deal with such issues as making moral decisions, Jesus, the Holy Spirit, creation and providence, salvation and discipleship, prayer, science and religion, and presenting the gospel.

GRAHAM SLATER AND C. S. RODD

vii

Introduction

This book is set out in two parts. Part One begins with five short chapters, each spelling out a pastoral problem relating to the sacrament of Baptism, while the remainder, rather longer chapters, attempt to tease out the theological and other issues which arise.

Part Two, which turns to Holy Communion, re-introduces the housegroup, with which readers of my *Worship* (number 2 in the present series, Epworth Press 1997) will already be familiar. In this part, all the chapters begin with a housegroup discussion which raises some of the key issues and continue with a section headed 'Reflections' in which they are explored in more detail. Questions for group discussion or individual consideration are provided at appropriate points.

The housegroup members and all the other 'contemporary' people referred to are products of my imagination, but I trust that their concerns and questions echo those which readers will themselves bring to the book.

It is extremely unlikely, however, that any reader will feel that I have dealt with, or even referred to, every important issue. Baptism and Holy Communion have, after all, been central to the life of the Christian church throughout its history, and an immense volume of literature has grown up around them. As a result, almost every paragraph of this little book could itself have become a book! I apologize, however, to any who find that I have ignored the very questions with which they hoped I would deal, and I hope that the books listed under 'Further Reading' (pp. 100–102) will be of some help to them, though, sadly, some of the titles are now out of print. In such cases it will be necessary to borrow them from a library, perhaps through the inter-library loans service.

From 1990 until 1998 I had the privilege of belonging to the committee which produced *The Methodist Worship Book*. The orders of Service for Holy Communion and Baptism in that book were first written by 'Group One'. My fellow members of that group were Martyn Atkins, Neil Dixon, Christine Odell and Norman Wallwork. From them I learned a great deal about sacramental theology and its liturgical expression. I dedicate this little book to them in the sure knowledge that they will find much in it with which to disagree.

MICHAEL J. TOWNSEND

Part 1

Baptism

1

A Difference Discovered

Helen and Marie were both students on a computer studies course at the local Further Education College. Helen had always lived locally, but Marie was a newcomer to the area, having moved with her parents a few months previously. They met by literally bumping into each other in the coffee bar on the first day, fell into conversation and quickly became firm friends.

One of the many things they discovered about each other in the course of long conversations was that they both went to church. 'We were all brought up as Catholics,' said Marie. 'Mum and Dad are very religious. Well, to be honest, I am too. I find it a great help to think that there is a God who cares for us and I always try to go to Mass on Sundays.' 'I was brought up as a Baptist,' said Helen. 'Dad is a deacon at our local church. And yes Marie, like you I don't just go to church on a Sunday because my parents expect me to. It really means something to me.'

But the major topic of conversation was Helen's forthcoming marriage to Dave, who belonged to the same church as she did. They had been engaged for some time and the wedding was planned to take place shortly before the computer studies course finished. Marie was very thrilled to be asked to be a bridesmaid and, when the time came, thoroughly enjoyed the experience. As she said to her mother later in the day, 'I don't think Baptists can be very different from us. The service was rather plain, but it was much the same as ours, really. And the Minister who married them was very sincere.'

When the course ended Marie and Helen kept in touch with each other, meeting at least once a week in the lunch hour. The day came when Helen had some exciting news to share with her friend. 'It's just been confirmed,' she told Marie, 'I'm pregnant.' 'Helen, how wonderful,' exclaimed Marie. 'When is

3

the baby due?' 'July 12th,' Helen replied. 'It does seem an awfully long way off.'

In the event, Ruth was born ten days early and Marie was one of the first visitors. 'Helen, she's absolutely gorgeous,' Marie enthused. 'And she's going to have the most enormous christening present from her auntie Marie, aren't you my love?' she said, addressing the baby. Helen looked puzzled. 'Christening present?' she queried. 'Yes,' said Marie excitedly. 'Have you fixed the date yet?' 'But,' responded Helen, 'We won't be having her christened. I thought you realized that.' It was Marie's turn to look puzzled. 'Won't be having her christened!' she repeated. 'But Helen, you and Dave are regular churchgoers, good Christians. In our family the christening is the very first thing we think about when a baby is born. My grandma wouldn't have me in her house until I'd been christened. I don't understand what you mean when you say you won't be having Ruth christened. What's stopping you?'

'Goodness me, Marie,' said Helen, 'We've talked about so many things I can't imagine why I've never told you about this. One of our distinctive beliefs as Baptists is that Christian baptism (which is really the proper name for christening) should be for believers – adults who can make their profession of faith in Jesus Christ – not for babies who can't know anything about it. We think that's what the New Testament tells us to do. I was baptized when I was fifteen and it was a great occasion in my life.'

'Well,' said Marie after a pause. 'I knew there were some differences between our churches, of course. But this one never even crossed my mind. When you asked me to be your bridesmaid I asked our priest to tell me something about the Baptist church, but he didn't seem to know very much. He simply said that you were Protestants, and I knew that already. Helen, this seems really strange to me. You see, I was brought up to believe that the baptism – we are taught to call it that too,

4

but old habits die hard – is the first thing you arrange for a baby; that if you are Christians you want to bring the baby into the family of the church as soon as possible. It doesn't seem right not to. And what about that bit in the Bible where Jesus talks about letting the little children come to him? Hasn't that got something to do with it?'

'I'm too tired to start discussing it with you now, Marie,' Helen replied, 'but we will talk about it sometime soon, I promise. And Ruth won't stay outside the family of the church, I can promise you that too. Dave and I will arrange a service of dedication, when we will thank God for giving her to us and promise to do our best as Christian parents. Obviously there won't be a christening cake or godparents, but there will definitely be a party afterwards. And if you want to give Ruth a dedication present, you most certainly can!' 'Thanks, Helen,' said Marie. 'I'd like to do that. But I still think you're wrong about not having her baptized.'

2

A Problem with the Vicar

Stuart and Kathy James first met each other at the church Youth Club, kept in touch during their time as students, and became engaged shortly after graduation. When they married they bought a house in a new estate on the other side of town, where most of the neighbours were young couples like themselves. In due course, planned and wanted, Charlotte was born.

'I've been thinking,' said Kathy one evening, 'We really ought to make arrangements to have Charlotte christened. She's six months old and we don't want her getting too heavy for the vicar to hold!' 'Funny you should say that,' Stuart responded. 'Mum only asked me last week whether we had thought about the christening. I think she would like it to be at St George's where she goes. 'No,' said Kathy. 'We belong here now and we ought to have the christening locally.' 'That would be St Michael's – Mickey's as Paul and Jane call it,' said Stuart. 'Well, it sounds a friendly kind of place from what we've heard about it – which is quite a lot!' Kathy smiled as she replied, 'Perhaps Jane and Paul will think their persistence has paid off at last.' Jane and Paul were Stuart and Kathy's next door neighbours and were deeply involved at Mickey's, as they called it. Paul played the keyboard at morning services and Jane led what they called Sunday Club. They often mentioned the church, saying how much they enjoyed what went on there and telling everyone about their lively and go-ahead young vicar, Tony.

So Kathy rang the vicarage and Stuart listened to her end of the conversation. 'Hello, is that the Reverend Ashton? I'm Kathy James from Elm Crescent. We've just had a baby, Charlotte – well, a while ago really, she's six months old now – and Stuart (he's my husband) and I were thinking we ought to get her christened before she gets too big. We were wondering,

6

would May 7th be all right for you? Oh . . . yes, I see. No, of course. I quite understand. We hadn't thought about that . . . Yes, a week tomorrow at half-past six will be fine. We look forward to meeting you then. Goodbye for now.'

'Problems?' enquired Stuart. 'No, not really,' said Kathy, 'It's just that when I asked about the date he said they don't take bookings for christenings over the phone. He wants to meet us at the vicarage to discuss things.' 'That's fine,' said Stuart. 'I hope he will go through the service with us. I like to know what I'm doing and what I have to say.'

Tony Ashton took them through to his study. 'Thank you both for coming,' he said. 'You rang me about Christian baptism for your daughter, Charlotte.' 'Yes,' said Kathy. 'Baptism is another name for christening is it, vicar?' 'Oh, please call me Tony, everyone does. Well, Kathy, in a way it is. But at St Michael's we call it baptism because that is the word which is used in the Bible. Now tell me why you want Charlotte to be baptized.' They thought for a moment, and then Stuart replied: 'I've been christened – sorry, I mean baptized – and so has Kathy. We both went to Sunday School at St George's when we were younger. Actually, my mother's still very regular there. And we were both brought up to believe that it's the right thing to do to have your baby, er baptized. Charlotte is special to us and we want her to have everything that's right.'

'I see,' said the vicar. 'Now think about this very carefully please. In the service I ask the parents: Do you turn to Christ? What does that mean to you?' Kathy replied, 'I'm not sure exactly. But it's all about being good Christian parents, isn't it? I mean, teaching Charlotte right from wrong, that kind of thing.' 'Well, that's a start,' said Tony Ashton. 'But there is a bit more to it than that, you know. The promises you have to make in the service are very serious ones.'

'Excuse me, vicar,' said Kathy, 'Are you saying that we're not really good enough to have our daughter christened?' 'No,

7

no, Kathy, of course not,' replied the vicar. 'But when we baptize young children we expect the parents to help them grow in the Christian faith in which they have been baptized. That's a very great responsibility.' 'I'm not sure what you're asking of us vicar,' said Stuart. 'Not asking, Stuart, offering – offering to help,' said Tony Ashton. 'Here at St Michael's we run special baptism preparation classes. There is an eight-week course and a fresh one starts at the beginning of next month. We meet on Thursday evenings.' 'What sort of thing goes on at these classes?' asked Stuart. 'They are run by my wife Janice and myself and two other young Christian couples,' was the reply. 'We usually begin with a time of prayer and praise. Then we look at a passage from the Bible which helps us to understand what it means to be Christian parents. I think you'd find it really helpful.' Kathy decided she had heard enough. She stood up suddenly. 'Well,' she said, 'Thank you for talking to us, vicar. We'll think it over and let you know.'

'It's a bit inconvenient,' said Stuart as they got into the car. 'If it takes eight weeks, we've missed the date we wanted.' 'Oh Stuart, that isn't the problem,' said Kathy crossly. 'The real problem is that the vicar doesn't think we're good enough Christians to have our daughter baptized unless we're prepared to go to those classes and listen to him and his wife rabbit on about the Bible. All we wanted to do was to take our Charlotte to church and ask God to bless her. You'd think the vicar would be glad about that, but instead we got all that rigmarole. I feel thoroughly patronized. No wonder the churches are empty if that's how they treat people. Don't you worry, when I next see Jane I shall tell her exactly what I think about her precious vicar and her wonderful Mickey's!'

'The question is, what do we do now?' said Stuart. 'Tell your Mum we'll be glad to go to St George's,' said Kathy. 'And hope the vicar there is a bit different from this one!'

3

A Problem in the Family

When Mary went round to her friend Phyllis for their usual Thursday morning cup of coffee she could see at once that Phyllis was upset about something. Eventually it was a simple question about Phyllis's daughter Jenny which produced an unexpected response. Jenny had married Darren a few years previously and they had gone to live at the other side of the country. They visited Phyllis quite often and she sometimes went to them for an extended stay. The relationship between them had always seemed very good, so when Mary asked, 'How are things with Jenny?' she was not really prepared for Phyllis to burst into tears.

'Why, Phyllis, whatever is the matter?' asked Mary. 'There's nothing wrong between her and Darren is there?' 'Oh no,' replied Phyllis, 'it's not them, it's Sean.' Sean was Darren and Jenny's baby son. He was just over two months old and Phyllis had recently returned from a week's visit to see her first grandchild. Friends, neighbours and everybody at church had been shown dozens of photographs. 'Is Sean ill?' asked Mary, 'He seemed fine when you were there last week.' 'No, it's nothing like that,' said Phyllis. 'Look, I'll make another cup of coffee and tell you about it. I do feel a bit silly giving way like that. I know it's nothing really, not compared with what some folks have to put up with. But it's worrying me to death and, to be honest, I would like to talk about it.' So Mary heard the story.

During the recent visit Phyllis had asked Jenny whether a date had been arranged for Sean's christening. Jenny's reply had been rather vague. She had talked about not having got round to it and about Darren not being quite sure what it was he really wanted. Phyllis wasn't happy with what she heard, but somehow it wasn't the right moment for pursuing the matter. It was only when she got home that Phyllis realized she was still

9

no wiser about the christening. So when her daughter rang one evening, Phyllis took the opportunity to raise the matter again. This time Jenny was more forthcoming.

'Look, Mum,' said Jenny, 'I know you won't like this, but Darren and I have decided we aren't going to have Sean christened.' Phyllis could hardly believe what she was hearing. 'Why ever not?' she asked. 'Everyone in our family has been christened. Your Dad and I had you christened when you were younger than Sean is now!' 'I know, Mum,' said Jenny, 'but it didn't do much good, did it? I mean, I never go to church and I haven't done for years.' This was true, and a source of genuine concern to Phyllis. Deep down she wondered whether it was one of the ways in which she had failed as a mother. 'I know you don't go to church,' Phyllis replied, 'but we had you christened and gave you the chance. Surely you can't deny little Sean the same chance as you had. It isn't fair!' 'I don't think there's anything unfair about it,' said Jenny. 'It's only a bit of water splashed on someone's head. What difference can that possibly make? If Sean wants to believe in God when he's older, well that's up to him; we won't stand in his way. But Darren says we would be hypocrites if we stood up in church and made all those promises, and I agree with him. So, sorry Mum, but no christening!' Phyllis had been much too upset to argue with Jenny any further and, in any case, there didn't seem much point. Her mind was obviously made up.

'So there you are, Mary,' said Phyllis. 'That's what's worrying me so much. I can't bear to think of Sean not being christened. It doesn't seem right somehow. I was brought up to believe that everybody should be christened. When a baby is christened it is as if we are saying that God loves that baby and has . . . well, sort of claimed it for his own, if you know what I mean. I may not be putting it very well, but that's how I feel about it. I think about that every time we have a christening in our church.' 'That's a beautiful thought,' said Mary, 'And I expect you're right. But you and I both know that God loves

10

Sean, because Jesus told us that God loves everyone. So it can't really mean that God loves him any the less just because Jenny and Darren have decided not to have him christened, can it?' 'I suppose not,' replied Phyllis. 'When you put it like that it doesn't seem very logical. But if it doesn't really matter whether or not Sean is christened, why do we christen babies at all? And if it does matter, and if Sean isn't christened and if, well, anything were to happen to him . . . Phyllis's voice tailed off.

Mary moved quickly to Phyllis's side and put her arm round her shoulder. 'Is that what's really worrying you, Phyllis? Are you frightened that if Sean isn't christened and if anything were to happen to him, as you put it, he might not go to heaven?' Phyllis nodded miserably and continued, 'I expect you think it's just an old wives' tale. But there are people who really believe that and, after all, we can't know for certain, can we?' Mary didn't know what to say, so she wisely said nothing. After quite a long period of silence Phyllis continued: 'I expect I shall get over it in time. But I do wish Darren and Jenny would change their minds. If they aren't prepared to make the promises, perhaps I could make them instead. Or perhaps we could have the christening here at our church and we could ask the minister to leave the promises out of the service. After all, it's the christening that matters, not what you say.' 'I don't know about that,' Mary answered, 'but I do know that we ought to have another talk about this next week.'

4

Philip Becomes a Problem

Methodist minister the Revd Colin Fox and his wife Susan cared very deeply about their son, Philip. Philip was born before Colin entered the ministry, and they were both aware of the pressures that are sometimes placed on ministers' children. Above all they were anxious that nothing should turn Philip against the Christian faith.

Fortunately, that did not seem to have happened. If anything the contrary seemed to be the case. The Sunday School at the first church to which Colin was appointed was extremely well run and there was never any difficulty in getting Philip to attend. By the time Colin moved to his second appointment Philip was through Sunday School. But the church had good young people's work and Philip quickly became involved. When he was fourteen he asked to be confirmed, which delighted both his parents. Sometimes Susan found herself wondering whether in due course Philip might not follow in his father's footsteps and enter the ministry. He certainly had a lively and enquiring mind and the meal table was often the place for astonishingly deep theological discussion.

Colin's third appointment was very different from the first two. He had been specially asked to take it, since it was a difficult situation and he was a very able minister. None of his new churches had any youth work, and there were very few members of the congregation under fifty. Right from the start Colin was plunged into a hectic schedule and, as a result, he hardly had time to think about how Philip was coping with a very different kind of church from anything he had known previously. Then one day Philip said casually, 'Dad, you know Mark and Terry?' Colin nodded. There seemed to be a fairly endless procession of teenagers through the Manse most evenings, but Mark and Terry were amongst the most presentable. 'What about them?' he asked. 'Well,' said Philip,

12

'They go to something called a 'Seekers Group' on Friday nights at the Living Stones Church on Sampson Road. They say it's really good and interesting and they want me to go with them. I can, can't I?' Colin frowned. The Living Stones Church was a breakaway from a local Baptist church. It had started up a couple of years previously, ironically in a disused Methodist church. Nobody seemed to know much about them other than that they had a keen young Pastor who had so far refused all invitations to attend the local Ministers' Meeting. Colin was wary. 'I'm not sure, Philip,' he began. Philip interrupted: 'Oh Dad, come on! It isn't as if we had a Youth Club at our church, and in any case church is so boring. This Seekers Group is especially for young Christians and Mark and Terry say it's really good.' 'I don't think we ought to object, Colin,' said Susan quickly. 'Philip's right in a way. We haven't anything to offer him. He can't come to much harm with Christian people, can he?'

So, very reluctantly, Colin agreed. For a few Fridays he tried to remember to ask Philip what the group had been doing that particular evening, but gave up worrying when Philip told him they'd had a Bible quiz or a talk on 'Christians and Drugs' or even, on one occasion, that they had been studying the Book of Job! So Colin stopped asking and Philip kept attending. It was some six months later that Philip dropped his bombshell.

'I've got something to tell you,' he said in the voice he reserved for special announcements. Susan and Colin waited. 'I'm going to be baptized at the beginning of March and I hope you'll come.' There was a stunned silence. Then Colin said, 'But Philip, you've been baptized! You were baptized by our minister, the Revd Arthur Wellesley when you were four months old.' 'No, Dad,' said his son, 'That was christening. That's what you do to babies. I'm going to be baptized properly, by total immersion, at the Living Stones Church.' Colin's voice rose: 'Who's been putting this nonsense into your head? Is it that Pastor?' Philip pondered: 'A bit, but it isn't

13

nonsense. We had a couple of evenings about it at the Seekers Group. When we looked at what the Bible says I realized our church does it all wrong. Baptism isn't for babies, it's for believers.' 'You really feel strongly about this, don't you?' Susan asked. 'Yes, I do. I feel that God is asking me to be baptized properly, as an act of witness. So I asked the Pastor about it and he said there was no problem.' 'No, there isn't a problem if you haven't been baptized already,' said Colin. 'But you've been baptized, and that's different. Does the Pastor know you've been baptized already?' 'Well,' Philip replied, 'I told him I'd been christened as a baby and he said that didn't count and I could have a proper baptism. I really mean it, Dad. I'm sorry if you don't like it, but I'm going ahead anyway. Oh, and Mark and Terry are being baptized at the same service.'

After Philip had left, Colin turned to his wife. 'Oh Susan,' he said, 'What are we going to do?'

5

Brenda Faces a Problem

Brenda Murray was enjoying her new job very much. She had been doing it for three months, and, not for the first time, marvelled at the way it had come about. It had taken her several years to discover her true vocation. She always felt she wanted to work with people and when she left school applied for entry into the nursing profession. She enjoyed her training, and afterwards found a job in a large teaching hospital. She was evidently happy and contented, so it was something of a surprise to the minister of the United Reformed church she attended when she told him that she thought God might be calling her into the ministry.

She put her call to the test, and was accepted for training. She was entered for a degree in theology which she secured with first-class honours. She was then called to a large URC pastorate where she spent seven happy and rewarding years. After that time a change seemed to be indicated, so she asked her Provincial Moderator to place her on the list of ministers looking for a new appointment. For over a year Brenda considered details of the various vacancies that were sent to her, but nothing seemed quite right. 'The trouble is,' she said to the Moderator, 'most of these look like more of the same. If I'm going to make a change, I want a fresh challenge.' The Moderator thought for a few minutes, 'What about hospital chaplaincy?' he asked. 'We need good ministers in those posts. Your previous experience would be helpful to you. I think you'd be a really effective chaplain.' This seemed a good idea to Brenda. She replied to an advertisement for a full-time hospital chaplaincy, and was duly appointed.

There was no doubt that she was enjoying her work, and she said as much to Jeremy, her Anglican colleague. 'This job's got everything,' she told him. 'I'm working with people all the time and I have marvellous discussions with the medical staff about some of the ethical dilemmas they face. Just take last week, for instance. I had two emergency baptisms in the maternity unit. I helped one of the junior nurses cope with the death of her mother. I was involved with the families of the three young people who had that horrific accident on the by-pass. I spent time with the partner of the young man on Ward 26 who has AIDS, and I had over an hour with the Medical Registrar exploring the ethical issues surrounding pain control and euthanasia. What a privileged life!'

At that moment Brenda's bleep sounded. 'It's Staff Nurse on Maternity, Brenda. Can you come over as quickly as possible please? A patient has asked for you.' When Brenda arrived she was shown into a side room. A young woman was sitting up in bed, with a young man perched uncomfortably at her side, his arm round her shoulders. Both were crying. They looked up as Brenda entered, and saw her clerical collar. The woman composed herself as best she could. 'I asked for the Chaplain. I hope you don't mind.' 'Of course not,' said Brenda with a smile. 'I'm Brenda, by the way. Is there some way I can help?' 'Yes, there is,' the woman replied. 'I'm Lorraine and this is Brian, my husband. We were expecting our first child and I was brought in last week because the doctors said there were complications. And, well, he was born a couple of hours ago, but he was dead.' Brenda started to say something, but Lorraine continued: 'No, let me finish please, because I've thought about what I want to say. You see, the same thing happened to my Mum, many years ago. In those days they handled things differently. Mum says they just took the child away. She didn't even see him. He didn't have a name, or a funeral, or anything. It has taken her years to get over it. Well, the nurses here have been ever so kind. I wanted to hold my baby, so I did – well, we both did. And they say we can have a proper little funeral service, in the hospital chapel if we want it, which we do.' 'Yes,' said Brian. 'That's what we both want. And we were going to call him Richard John if it was a boy. So we want you

16

to christen him please, so that he's got a name at the service. You will, won't you?'

Brenda had never felt so helpless in her life. She knew she needed to talk to someone. She took a deep breath. 'I can't say how sorry I am about what has happened,' she said. 'But I honestly don't know what to say about a christening. I've never been faced with this before. I need a little time to think, but I promise I'll come back to you very soon and we'll talk about it then.' So, after she had stayed a while longer and said a short prayer, Brenda sped back to the Chaplaincy Office hoping that Jeremy would still be there. He was, and Brenda told him the story. 'I simply don't know what to do!' she exclaimed. 'My understanding of the sacrament of baptism tells me that I cannot possibly baptize someone who is dead. And yet the young couple are so distressed and so determined. They think that, if the baby is baptized, he will have a name; and that's important to them. They're suffering enough as it is, and if I tell them I can't do it, that will seem so uncaring. My head is telling me one thing, but my heart is telling me something else. I tell you, Jeremy, I wish I'd never taken this job. What am I to do?'

17

6

The Origins of Christian Baptism

Even in an age when the proportion of the population being baptized is falling, a baptism is still a reasonably frequent occurrence in many churches. It is easy for us to take its existence for granted. Baptism in water is, it might seem, simply the form which the rite of Christian initiation takes. But how did it come about that the church chose this particular rite rather than some other one?

Almost all baptismal services include these words of the risen Christ from Matthew's Gospel: 'All authority in heaven and on earth has been given to me. Go therefore and make disciples of all nations, baptizing them in the name of the Father and of the Son and of the Holy Spirit . . . ' (Matthew 28.18–19). Most biblical scholars think that this language has been shaped by the experience of the early Christians and may reflect the formula which came to be used in baptism. This is even more likely to be the case with Mark 16.16, which records the risen Christ as saying: 'The one who believes and is baptized will be saved.' Yet even if, as most scholars judge, this was not originally part of Mark's Gospel, it still bears witness to the way in which, from its earliest days, the Christian church practised baptism and believed that by so doing it was acting in obedience to Christ's command.

The Acts of the Apostles supplies the evidence that to be baptized was the automatic next step for anyone who believed the Christian message, and that considerable significance was given to such baptism. After Peter had preached his sermon to the crowd on the first Day of Pentecost, he was asked what his hearers should do next and replied, 'Repent, and be baptized every one of you in the name of Jesus Christ . . . '(Acts 2.38). We are told that 'those who welcomed his message were baptized' and thereby became members of the Christian community (Acts 2.41).

When Philip met the Ethiopian official on the road from Jerusalem to Gaza and explained to him the good news about Jesus, the Ethiopian at once asked for baptism, and received it (Acts 8.35–39). After Saul, chief persecutor of the Christian cause, was converted on the road to Damascus, he went to the house of Ananias the Christian where he was baptized (Acts 9.18). At the conversion of Cornelius and his household the pattern was slightly different. As Peter was preaching to them, the Holy Spirit came upon his hearers and they began to show evidence of this. The members of Cornelius' household were amongst the first Gentile converts to the new faith. There was understandable doubt amongst some Jewish Christians about whether Gentiles could become Christians without becoming Jews first. The clear evidence in this story that such converts had already received the Spirit dispelled such doubts. It did not though, make baptism with water superfluous. Quite the contrary: Peter used the fact that they had received the Spirit as evidence that they *could* now be baptized in water (Acts 10.47–48). Acts does not record the baptism of every convert, but it was evidently taken for granted. We can see this from the unselfconscious way in which Luke says of Lydia, 'When she and her household were baptized . . . ' (Acts 16.15).

Some of the New Testament letters simply assume that Christian readers will have been baptized. The Letter to the Hebrews even lists 'instructions about baptism' as part of the basic teaching they have received and on which they need no longer dwell as they press on towards greater maturity (Hebrews 6.2). When Paul rebukes his converts in the Corinthian church for their tendency to divide into factions, he reminds them that they were baptized not in his name, but in the name of Christ. Indeed, he cannot quite remember which of them he has baptized, and comments, 'For Christ did not send me to baptize but to proclaim the gospel . . . (I Corinthians 1.17). Paul is not intending to devalue baptism or to discourage it. The picture is of Paul as a visiting evangelist happy, for the most part, to leave the actual baptizing of those converted through his preaching to the local ministry of the church. Baptism is here portrayed as a normative part of the settled pattern of congregational life.

Why did baptism evidently form part of the Christian community's life from the earliest days? Or, to put it another way, when the apostles were asked on the first Day of Pentecost what people should do in response to Peter's sermon, how did Peter know that the proper reply was, 'Repent and be baptized . . . ?'

At one level, the association of some kind of water ceremony with repentance, purification, conversion and a new way of life seems fairly obvious. Just as washing in water makes us physically clean, so washing in a particular way (ritual washing), perhaps accompanied by prayer or other set words, may be thought to make us ceremonially or ritually clean. We know that a number of religions in the Graeco-Roman world at the time of Jesus used water ceremonies in this way. Indeed, the Jewish religion itself (and we remember that the disciples, like Jesus himself, were all Jews) prescribed such ritual washings under certain circumstances. The Gospels sometimes record Jesus criticizing the way in which correct performance of these rituals could become a substitute for holy living (see Mark 1.1–8). But such ritual washings are quite different from baptism in a number of ways and their existence does not directly help us to understand how and why the Christian church practised baptism from its earliest days. We have to say that we do not know for certain why this happened, but there are some possible indications, again from Jewish sources.

In the first place, we have some evidence from what are sometimes called 'Jewish sects' (such as the Qumran community which probably bequeathed us the famous Dead Sea Scrolls), that their members engaged in ceremonial washing, with the intention of making themselves morally, rather than ritually, clean. They were looking forward to a new

20

moral and religious order and wanted to be part of it. Some scholars judge that the practices of such communities had an important influence on the work of John the Baptist and, through him, on Jesus and the first Christians. This seems highly likely, but we cannot be absolutely sure about it.

In the second place, we know about what is often called 'proselyte baptism'. There is good evidence that when people converted to the Jewish faith, in addition to being circumcised (if they were men), they and their entire family took a ritual bath. This signified entry into a new life in which they would keep the requirements of the Jewish Law. Most scholars believe that these Jewish proselyte baptisms were a major influence on the infant church, though we cannot be certain about this. The first solid evidence for them dates from the Christian era, though the practice itself may have been earlier.

We are on firmer ground when we turn to the work of John the Baptist. The Synoptic Gospels agree that what he offered was a 'baptism of repentance for the forgiveness of sins' (Mark 1.4; Matthew 3.1–6; Luke 3.3). John's Gospel describes messengers from the Pharisees asking John about the purpose of his baptisms and being told, 'I baptize with water. Among you stands one whom you do not know' (John 1.26). This rather mysterious reply is almost immediately amplified: 'I came baptizing with water for this reason, that he (Jesus) might be revealed to Israel' (John 1.31). The activities of John the Baptist make two things clear. Firstly, water baptism clearly stands for a relationship between repentance and forgiveness, an old life and a new life. Secondly, through such baptisms people were being prepared to receive Jesus and his message and recognize him for who he was (Luke 7.29–30 offers further testimony to this).

John's baptizing ministry did not come to an end when Jesus began his own ministry of preaching and healing, but continued alongside it. So strong was the association between the two in the popular mind, that after John's death some people were

21

reported as thinking that Jesus might be John restored to life (Mark 9.28). John's Gospel hints that at an early stage of his ministry Jesus himself baptized others (John 3.25), but almost immediately qualifies the statement (John 4.2). The other Gospels give no hint that Jesus baptized. He seems to have regarded that as John's ministry, not his. But it was nevertheless work on which his own ministry could be built. Given this, we can begin to understand how the disciples would regard it as perfectly natural that anyone coming to repentance and faith should be baptized.

There is also the remarkable fact that Jesus himself was baptized by John (Mark 1.9–11; Matthew 3.13–17; Luke 3.21–22). From early times this story caused the church some embarrassment, simply because if Jesus was sinless, as Christians claimed, why should he need the baptism of repentance for the forgiveness of sins, which John offered? Perhaps this is one reason why in John's Gospel – the last of the four to be written – this story does not appear. It is clearly implied in John 1.29–34, but not spelled out. Instead, Jesus' superiority to John and his work is stressed. The story need not cause us embarrassment now. John called people to be obedient to God. For sinful human beings this meant repentance and a new beginning. For Jesus, as he stood on the threshold of his public ministry, it meant affirming his obedience to his Father's will, knowing that that would mean a hard road ahead of him. Against this background, we can begin to understand how the disciples would have regarded it as natural that anyone coming to a new obedience to God should be baptized.

From this brief survey of the New Testament evidence we can see that the first Christians practised baptism as a matter of course and believed that, by so doing, they were acting in obedience to Christ's command. It is highly likely, though not certain, that the earliest Christian baptisms took place simply in the name of Jesus. This is what is described in Acts 8.16 and 10.48. It may also be the implication of Paul's phrasing in

I Corinthians 3.13b, and may lie behind other New Testament references such as James 2.7. But by the time Matthew's Gospel came to be written the church had begun to think through the implications of what had happened for human salvation and to see within those events the work of the one God, who is Father, Son and Holy Spirit. And so the Great Commission of Matthew's Gospel commands baptism in the name of the Trinity (Matthew 28.19). This has been the practice of the Christian church ever since.

Baptism, then, marks the beginning of Christian discipleship. Repentance, faith and baptism belong together in the New Testament as part of one act. It is the sacrament of entry into the faith community. Although the style and manner of baptism has varied greatly through the succeeding centuries, all mainstream Christian churches have continued to practise it and have recognized that those who have been properly baptized have not just joined a branch of the church, but have been initiated into the fellowship of the church universal.

For discussion

In the light of the practice of the early church, how would you answer Phyllis's daughter, Jenny, who said, 'It's only a bit of water splashed on someone's head.'?

The Meaning of Christian Baptism

If it is from the Acts of the Apostles that we learn most about the early church's practice of baptism, it is from some of the New Testament letters that we discover what the first Christians thought actually happened when someone was baptized. Various images are used, but taken together they amount to this: *Through baptism we are united with Christ and share in the salvation he brought to the world.* We need to explore a little further the images which point to this conclusion.

1. *Clothed with Christ.*

In Galatians 3.27 Paul writes: 'As many of you as were baptized into Christ Jesus have clothed yourselves with Christ.' It is generally thought that this vivid image is derived from the custom of putting on new robes straight after the baptismal ceremony. Paul is reminding his readers that through baptism they have come into a new relationship with their risen and living Lord. Their baptism was 'into Christ Jesus', that is to say, they now belong to Christ through their baptism. This verse is part of a passage in which Paul is arguing that all Christian people, regardless of other differences between them, have the common status of children of God.

2. *Buried with Christ.*

In Romans 6.3–4a Paul writes: 'Do you not know that all of us who have been baptized into Christ Jesus were baptized into his death? Therefore we have been buried with him by baptism into death . . . ' Here again we have a reminder that baptism is 'into' Christ, but Paul makes a different point from the one in Galatians. Here he is concerned to show why Christians can no longer continue to live sinful lives. They cannot do so because, as verse 2 puts it, they have 'died to sin'. And how have they died to sin? By being baptized into Christ's death, which brought the forgiveness of sins. The Gospels record Jesus himself making the link between the imagery of baptism and his forthcoming sufferings and death (Mark 10.35–40; Luke 12.50).

Here Paul tells his readers that, because Christ died in order to overcome sin, those who belong to him through baptism effectively share in that death and all the benefits that it has brought. This does not mean, of course, that those who have been baptized have become incapable of sin! But they do not *belong* to evil and sin any more; rather, they belong to Christ. The task of Christian discipleship is always that of becoming in daily practice what God's grace has made us, which is why in this passage Paul still needs to urge his readers not to sin. But this is now possible since not only are they 'dead to sin', they are also 'alive to God in Christ Jesus' (6.11). This is what baptism has done for us, and this spiritual reality, the New Testament suggests, has to be claimed and lived out day by day by each baptized person.

3. *Raised with Christ.*

After saying that we have been buried with Christ in baptism, Paul goes on to say: ' . . . so that, just as Christ was raised from the dead by the glory of the Father, so we too might walk in newness of life. For if we have been united with him in a death like his, we will certainly be united with him in a resurrection like his.' (Romans 6. 4b–5). If Christ conquered sin through his death and he conquered death though his rising, then those who are united with him through baptism share in both these victories. But there is a difference between the two! When Paul writes about sharing in the resurrection life of Christ, he does so in the future tense. This, it seems, is something which *will* happen to us, but it has not happened yet. In the meantime, as baptized people, we are encouraged to walk in 'newness of life'. This phrase (familiar to many from the confession in the *Sunday*

25

Service) is a description of the life of the baptized. This new life, in which they now share, is in turn to be shaped and transformed by the knowledge that its ultimate goal is life with Christ.

4. *United with Christ's people.*

In I Corinthians 12.13 Paul writes: 'For in the one Spirit we were all baptized into one body.' Some scholars think this is a reference to what is sometimes called 'baptism in the Spirit', rather than water-baptism, but this is unlikely. The New Testament picture is mixed. Where baptism in the Spirit is referred to, it sometimes precedes baptism in water and sometimes follows it. The most natural way to interpret Paul here is that the Holy Spirit can be thought of as the active agent in baptism. However that may be, the key phrase is about being baptized into one body. There are many New Testament pictures of the church, but 'the body of Christ' is one of the most profound and important. Paul may have developed this understanding because of the rivalries and antagonisms which existed between different groups within the Corinthian church. In I Corinthians 12 (and in Romans 12) he stresses both the diversity (there are lots of different gifts) and the unity (there is only one source) of the Holy Spirit's work. His conclusion, in I Corinthians 12.27, is: 'Now you are the body of Christ and individually members of it' (compare Romans 12.5). As individual Christians are baptized into Christ's death and resurrection, they thereby become part of Christ's body on earth, which is the church. This is why the great appeal for unity in Ephesians can include baptism as one of the unifying factors: 'There is one body and one Spirit, just as you were called to the one hope of your calling, one Lord, one faith, one baptism, one God and Father of all . . . ' (Ephesians 4.4–6). This is why we call baptism 'Christian initiation'. Those who are baptized do not simply receive a private blessing; they become part of the Christian community. This has further implications. We may say that to share in the body of Christ is to share in the salvation he brought to the world in another sense than just personally benefiting from it. The church is called to be the active agent of Christ's ministry in the world today and so, when we become part of it through baptism, we also become part of that ministry.

Even though Christ's body, the church, is at present divided in so many ways, nobody is ever baptized into a *denomination,* as an Anglican, a Catholic, a Lutheran or a Methodist. Baptism is the sacrament of entry into the world-wide faith community. In recent years the different denominations have re-affirmed their acceptance of baptisms in one another's churches (except, of course, for those who do not accept the validity of any infant baptism) and many baptismal certificates carry a list of those churches which will accept them as evidence of valid baptism. There is only one body, fragmented though it may presently be. Nor, if baptism is initiation into the Christian community, can it be regarded as a purely private matter, involving only the individual concerned and the immediate family. When someone becomes a member of the body of Christ, the rest of the body has responsibilities towards him or her. As a sign of this, it has become customary in many churches for the newly baptized to be taken into the midst of the worshipping congregation so that all present can acknowledge the new relationship.

The four images of baptism which we have explored all come from the fertile mind of the apostle Paul. There are two other important references which need to be considered.

Firstly, in I Peter 3.20, the author refers to the Old Testament story of Noah and the flood, about which he says that those aboard the ark were saved 'through water'. This leads him in the next verse to say to his Christian readers: 'and baptism . . . now saves you – not as a removal of dirt from the body, but as an appeal to God for a good conscience, through the resurrection of Jesus Christ . . . ' This is not a particularly easy passage to interpret, but it may be paraphrased along these lines: Just as God saved Noah and his family, so God saves people now through baptism, because those who come for baptism do so with a desire to be set free from sin and God, who raised Jesus from the dead, will honour this.

Secondly, John 3.5 has been taken by some to be a direct reference to baptism: 'Jesus answered, "Very truly, I tell you, no one can enter the kingdom of God without being born of water and the Spirit."' If this is about baptism, it asserts the absolute necessity of such baptism for salvation, something which the New Testament does nowhere else. Also, since Christian baptism had not yet been instituted, it is difficult to know what Nicodemus, to whom these words were addressed, could have made of them. On balance it is very unlikely that baptism is in view here, though it is understandable how later Christian readers, convinced of the importance of baptism, should have read it back into this text.

Our necessarily brief and rather selective examination of New Testament teaching about baptism may have produced at least one surprise: it makes very little use of the imagery of *washing*. There are some places where this may be in mind (e.g. I Corinthians 6.11), but it is certainly not prominent. Instead, the emphasis is on the way in which Christians are united to Christ in baptism, sharing in his death and resurrection and therefore in the salvation from sin he came to bring and – at some point in the future – in his glory too. Because in baptism we are united with Christ, we are also made members of his body, the church. These are not so much things we do as things which God does for us, and they are admirably summed up in the prayer over the water in the baptismal services in *The Methodist Worship Book*:

> Pour out your Holy Spirit
> that those baptized in this water
> may die to sin,
> be raised with Christ,
> and be born to new life in the family of your Church.

For discussion

In the light of the New Testament teaching about what baptism means, is it (a) essential, (b) desirable, (c) optional, or (d) unnecessary for a Christian believer to be baptized?

8

For Believers Only?

There are some deep divisions within and between the Christian churches about who may appropriately be baptized. The issues are both theological and pastoral, and they occur in a number of different contexts. The most obvious one is whether baptism should be administered only to those who confess a personal faith in Christ – who will normally be adults – or whether it is also right to baptize young children. Some denominations (Baptist churches, Brethren fellowships, Pentecostalist churches and most Independent and House churches) only administer baptism on profession of faith. They are in the minority. Most mainstream Christian denominations believe it is right to baptize young children as well.

Marie was quite shocked when her Baptist friend Helen told her that, as a deliberate choice, her new baby would not be baptized. As a good Catholic, Marie had been brought up to believe that the baptism is the first thing a family should arrange for a new baby. Her position was clear: 'If you are Christians, you want to bring the baby into the family of the church as soon as possible.' Helen's insistence that baptism is only for those who can make their profession of faith in Jesus Christ because 'that's what the New Testament tells us to do' was a challenge to everything Marie believed about the nature of Christian discipleship. Which of them was right?

The New Testament evidence appears at first to be perfectly straightforward. As we saw in Chapter 6, baptism was conferred on those who, having responded to the preaching of the gospel, confessed their faith in Christ and became part of the community which followed him. It would seem that the first recorded baptisms were of believing adults, and that is exactly what we would expect. In the nature of the case it could hardly have been otherwise. That situation has been repeated every time Christian missionaries have gone to a new place which has not heard the gospel before. But is this simply a historical fact, or is it also a theological principle? And is the biblical evidence quite as clear as it seems at first sight?

When, on the Day of Pentecost, Peter instructed those who responded to his preaching on what to do next, he told them to 'Repent, and be baptized every one of you in the name of Jesus Christ' (Acts 2.38). But he went on immediately: 'For the promise is for you, for your children, and for all who are far away . . . '(Acts 2.39). It is at this point that we need to remember the significance of the family for the ancient world in general and for the Jewish community in particular. Children were certainly included in proselyte baptism. More importantly, we may see a parallel with the practice of circumcision. When circumcision was first instituted as the mark of God's covenant with Abraham, it was specifically said to apply to all members of his household, children included (Genesis 17.10–14). The parallel between circumcision and baptism is, of course, far from exact, not least because circumcision was confined to males and baptism is for women as well. Some scholars refuse to acknowledge any connection between the two. The essential point, though, is that they both mark a relationship between God and God's people. It would therefore be entirely natural for the first Christian converts – who all came from a Jewish background – to ask, 'What is the place of our children in this new covenant that God is making with us?'

There are, in fact, several passages in the New Testament which suggest that children were probably included in baptisms. The first comes when Peter visits Cornelius: he and his colleagues witness the Holy Spirit being poured out upon those who hear his message and the water baptism follows immediately (Acts 10.44–48). When Peter later made his report about this to the Christians in Jerusalem he told them of Cornelius' expectation that his 'entire household' would be saved (Acts 11.14). The clear meaning of this phrase is that it includes all who were regarded as being part of the Roman *familia* – slaves and other dependants as well as those whom we think of as 'family' in the narrower sense. It would be extraordinary if such a household did not include children. Equally striking is the account of how the Philippian jailer came to faith, where we read: ' ... he and his entire family were baptized without delay' (Acts 16.33). There is also the unselfconscious reference to the baptism of Lydia's household (Acts 16.15) already referred to; and Paul, trying to recall exactly whom he had baptized in Corinth, does remember that he baptized 'the household of Stephanas' (I Corinthians 1.16).

Even at the level of the New Testament texts, therefore, it seems impossible to sustain the claim that in the beginning Christian baptism was administered only to believing adults. True, there is no command to baptize children anywhere in the New Testament, but equally there is no command to refrain from doing so! The pattern of events seems to be closely reflected in the Great Commission of Matthew 28.19–20: *first* make disciples (and children are not excluded), then baptize them and *after that* teach them.

Yet those who argue for the rightness of baptizing young children would not rest their case simply on what we can deduce from the New Testament about earliest Christian practice, important though that is. They would also say that the baptism of infants demonstrates in very clear terms the absolute heart of the Christian gospel. When Paul writes in Romans 6.8, 'God proves his love for us in that while we still were sinners Christ died for us', he encapsulates the essential meaning and movement of the Christian Good News. The God who has revealed himself in Jesus Christ does not wait for us to repent of our sins and return to him before he loves us. On the contrary, he goes in search of what has gone astray and rejoices to find it (Luke 15.1–7). Not only has Christ died for us, he has done so before we could ever know about it and most certainly before we could deserve it. Our salvation is not something we could ever have done for ourselves, nor does it depend on our goodness, our moral worth or our deserving characters. On the contrary, it is 'Love to the loveless shown / that they might lovely be', as Samuel Crossman's hymn famously puts it. That being so, what finer demonstration of that truth could there be than infant baptism? In such baptisms, God's love is declared and poured out upon those who know nothing about it, have done nothing to deserve it and cannot, in that moment, do anything to respond to it. How much clearer could it be made that the salvation of human beings is God's initiative and God's activity? Of course, there is the danger of forgetting that God's initiative seeks a human response. But there is at least an equal danger, if baptism is restricted to believers, of turning it into no more than a human work, something we do, and offer to God. When we baptize young children, we declare that God's grace in Christ comes first and we (usually meaning 'parents and congregation') pledge ourselves to work and pray for the response to come as the child grows up. The importance of maintaining the priority of God's initiative in our salvation is captured by some words which may be addressed to the baptismal candidates, now found in *The Methodist Worship Book*. They are believed to originate from the French Reformed tradition, but come in this form from the Uniting Church in Australia Assembly Commission on Liturgy. They run:

> for you Jesus Christ came into the world;
> for you he lived and showed God's love;
> for you he suffered death on the Cross;
> for you he triumphed over death,
> rising to newness of life;
> for you he prays at God's right hand:
>   all this for you,
>   before you could know anything of it.
> In your baptism,
> the word of Scripture is fulfilled:
> 'We love, because God first loved us.'

These words may be said at the baptism of those able to answer for themselves as well as at the baptism of infants, for they are equally true in that situation. God's grace always has priority.

For discussion

The case outlined in this chapter is (a) that the New Testament evidence allows for the baptism of children, and (b) that the nature of Christian gospel positively encourages it. Do you find this case convincing? Should the biblical evidence determine our decision on this question, or are there other factors to be considered?

9

For Whose Children?

There are clearly some enormous differences between the situation of New Testament times and ours today. In the early days of the church the overwhelming majority of baptisms would indeed have been of believing adults, whereas today most baptisms that take place are of young children. This change came about gradually as the Christian faith spread and gained in influence. By the end of the fourth century it was, in effect, the established religion of the Roman Empire. The higher the proportion of the population which claimed, at least nominally, to be Christian, the greater the number of children presented for baptism. In this way, the baptism of infants comes to be seen as, in practice, the 'normal' thing to do, with the baptism of believing adults as the exception. Even though in this century we have begun to see a reversal of this trend – 'the end of Christendom' as it has been called – with a consequential decline in the number of requests for infant baptism, such baptism continues to be thought of as normal. This leaves many Christians, in all the mainstream churches, feeling somewhat uncomfortable.

So the question of who should be baptized is not wholly straightforward. Some people contend that only the children of practising Christians should be baptized, whilst others argue that when any parents request baptism for their children it should never be refused. The arguments are very complex and people's stance is often about more than their view of baptism itself. It also involves their understanding of the nature of the church and what it means to be a Christian disciple.

Stuart and Kathy James could well be thought of as 'nominal Christians'. They requested baptism for their daughter because they had been baptized themselves as infants and brought up in the church and because, as caring parents, they wanted her to 'have everything that's right', as Stuart expressed it. This

35

expectation clashed with the vicar's perception of what baptism was all about. He clearly took the view that parents who brought their children for baptism should themselves be practising, not just nominal, Christians. He tried to use the promises which the parents make in the baptismal service to explore the depth and reality of Kathy and Stuart's faith and expected them to attend both Sunday worship and baptismal preparation classes in order to understand what it means to be a Christian parent. Stuart and Kathy James saw his attitude as patronizing and felt that they had experienced rejection. But was Tony Ashton's baptismal policy (as opposed perhaps to his somewhat unhelpful attitude) really so unreasonable?

In recent years a great deal of concern has been expressed about what is sometimes called 'indiscriminate baptism', where the churches have been willing to baptize any young child brought to them without asking any questions about what such a ceremony might mean, or whether there is any real commitment to Christian faith and discipleship on the part of the parents. Some people have described this situation as a scandal. One of the most important ecumenical publications of our time came from the World Council of Churches Faith and Order Commission meeting in Lima, Peru in 1982. It was published under the title *Baptism, Eucharist and Ministry*. In the section on baptism we find these words: 'In many large European and North American majority churches infant baptism is often practised in an apparently indiscriminate way. This contributes to the reluctance of churches which practise believers' baptism to acknowledge the validity of infant baptism; this fact should lead to more critical reflection on the meaning of baptism within those majority churches themselves.'

There are those who would defend totally indiscriminate infant baptism, not only on the grounds that it offers the churches pastoral and evangelistic opportunities (and avoids the feeling of rejection which can otherwise be felt by some parents) but on theological grounds. They would argue that since the love of God is entirely undiscriminating, baptism, which declares and expresses it, must be offered on the same basis. This is a powerful and important argument. Christians undoubtedly do worship a God who, as made known to us in Christ, loves without distinction. There is indeed a danger that a 'rigorist' baptismal practice can convey the message that some parents are 'not good enough' to have their children baptized, as Kathy James expressed it. That, in turn, can be heard as saying that they are not good enough to be loved by God. No Christian could possibly defend that view. The difficulty is, however, that although baptism does indeed declare the love of an undiscriminating God, there is *more* to the meaning of baptism than that, as we have already seen. If baptism is initiation into the Christian community, involving dying and rising with Christ, why should anyone wish their child to be initiated in that way if Christian faith and life means nothing to them?

In fact, the baptismal liturgies of most churches make it plain that baptism is administered on profession of faith. One slightly unfortunate feature of the baptismal services in the *Methodist Service Book* (1975) was that the section of the service immediately before the actual baptism was called 'The Promises and the Profession of Faith'. This made it appear to some that the issue was whether or not parents could realistically make the promises and, if they could not, to argue that the baptism should not take place. The Anglican *Alternative Service Book 1980* rite for the baptism of children has no promises as such, but a strong section preceding the baptism called 'The Decision' which begins: 'Those who bring children to be baptized must affirm their allegiance to Christ . . . ' A profession of faith, in a Trinitarian form, is required immediately before the baptism. All the baptismal services in *The Methodist Worship Book* (1999) deliberately separate the 'Affirmation of Faith' which takes place before the baptism, from the Promises, which take place after it. This makes it very clear that, as in the New Testament, the baptism takes place on the basis of expressed repentance and faith. Indeed, the wording of the Promises in the service for the Baptism of Young Children stresses that, far from being a precondition for baptism, they are a response to it. The minister says:

> I ask you now to respond
> to God's love and grace to your *children*
> by making these promises.

In effect, these baptismal liturgies place the responsibility for making sure that the profession of faith is sincerely made on those who make them. It can certainly be argued that when parents have been asked (to quote the words of *The Methodist Worship Book*):

> Do you turn to God,
> trusting in Jesus Christ as Lord and Saviour,
> and in the Holy Spirit as Helper and Guide?

and have publicly stated, 'By the grace of God, I do', the baptism which follows is hardly indiscriminate! The real issue may then be what many parents *understand* by the profession of faith which they are required to make. Certainly it is reasonable for the church to help them understand the meaning and implications of what they will say (though hopefully in a rather less off-putting way than that adopted by the Revd Tony Ashton). But is it not reasonable for us to at least begin from the position that, if we have given them the appropriate help, we must then trust their integrity?

38

For discussion

Do you think your church practices 'indiscriminate baptism' and, if so, do you think this is a 'scandal'? How can the church best help parents who bring their children for baptism to understand the faith they will be asked to profess?

10

Unbaptized?

Whatever view the churches take about how they should respond to requests for infant baptism from parents who are not themselves regular worshippers, there are many fewer such requests than once there were. A good many people now becoming parents have not themselves been baptized. Others may have been baptized, but have no effective contact with a church and so see no good reason for seeking baptism for their children. Sometimes in this situation there may be pressure from older members of the family, especially grandparents. This was the situation for Phyllis, whose daughter and son-in-law decided that since they did not themselves go to church they would be hypocrites if they made promises in church which they had no intention of keeping. Although a decline in the numbers of infant baptisms is usually interpreted by the media as yet another sign of the overall decline of the church, it may in fact represent a greater willingness to be honest on the part of those who know that they cannot call themselves Christians in any meaningful sense.

In the mid 1970s I was telephoned by a man who wanted to know whether I would be willing to baptize his child. He continued: 'Both of us are atheists, but we want to give her every opportunity in life and, if you're willing to do it, we don't mind.' When I explained to him that, if both parents were atheists, they could not possibly make the necessary profession of faith with any integrity and that I didn't think it was the church's job to encourage dishonesty, he replied, 'That's fine by me. And she won't suffer by not being baptized, will she?' I assured him that the God in whom I believed – though he did not – loved his daughter whether or not she was baptized, and that seemed to satisfy him.

Some people, who would not consciously accept the truth of the Christian faith for themselves, nevertheless find that some fragments of what Christians believe (or, more likely, what Christians are *thought* to believe) are present in their subconscious and come to the surface at particular times. We may judge that was in the mind of my telephone caller when he asked, 'She won't suffer by not being baptized, will she?' Much the same thought was in Phyllis's mind, concerning her grandson, Sean. She at first expressed her anxiety by saying that, when a baby is baptized, it means that God has 'claimed it for his own.' Given a little more time, she admitted that, deep down, she was worried that, if Sean died unbaptized, he might not go to heaven. Such anxieties might be very real because concern for the welfare of a human infant touches very deep chords in most people. But where does the idea that unbaptized children might not go to heaven come from in the first place? As we have seen, the New Testament, although it regards baptism as natural and normative, does not regard it as *essential* to salvation (unless we take a particular, and rather unlikely, view of John 3.5).

In the mediaeval period theologians engaged in a great deal of speculation about the condition of those who had died, what was happening to them and what might yet happen. With the love of systematization that was characteristic of those days, they divided the souls of the departed into five groups. The fourth of these was called *limbus infantium* from which we get the word 'limbo'; and it was in 'limbo' that the souls of infants who had died unbaptized were said to dwell. It was thought that they could not go to heaven, because they had been born in original sin which had not been washed away by baptism. But neither would they go to hell, because they had not consciously sinned. So limbo was thought of as a place of nothingness, neither heaven nor hell. It can hardly be imagined that there is a serious theologian today who would support this kind of thinking. It has no basis whatever in any New Testament teaching. Indeed, it seems to directly contradict what we know of the attitude of Jesus towards little children. We recall that when people brought little children to Jesus for his blessing, the disciples at first tried to stop them. Mark continues: 'But when Jesus saw this, he was indignant and said to them, "Let the little children come to me; do not stop them; for it is to such as these that the kingdom of God belongs. Truly I tell you, whoever does not receive the kingdom of God as a little child will never enter it." And he took them up in his arms, laid his hands on them, and blessed them' (Mark 10.14–16). And, of course, the children about whom Jesus said, 'it is to such as these that the kingdom of God belongs' were unbaptized, since Christian baptism did not yet exist!

Put simply: if Christians believe that in Jesus Christ we see what God is like, then in Jesus' attitude to little children we see God's attitude to them too. If Mary had a further talk with Phyllis about her fears, she would have done well to point to the biblical images of Jesus with children in his arms as well as reminding her that 'Jesus told us that God loves everyone'.

For discussion

How would you attempt to help someone whose baby had died without being baptized, and who was worried about what would happen to him or her?

11

Rebaptized?

When Philip Fox told his parents that he was going to be baptized his father protested, 'But, Philip, you've been baptized!' In his reply, Philip drew a sharp distinction between 'christening', which he said is for babies, and 'baptism' which is for believing adults such as himself. He was encouraged in this attitude by the pastor at the Living Stones Church, who told him that his 'christening' as a baby did not count.

Many ministers have, in recent years, become familiar with the request by young people, and sometimes older people too, to be baptized as believers when they have already been baptized in infancy. Often this is the result, as it was in Philip's case, of their coming into contact with a 'lively' church which only baptizes believers and contrasting this with their own 'dead' church which baptizes infants but does not appear to make many converts to Christianity in the process.

Language can be a slippery thing! It is not unknown for people requesting believer's baptism, on being asked whether they have been baptized before to say, 'No,' and then add, 'but I was christened as a baby.' Indeed, Philip came very close to saying this. In part this may be the church's fault for allowing it to appear that the baptism of those who are able to answer for themselves and the baptism of young children are two different things. Although the word 'christen' is perfectly acceptable in terms of its original meaning, its popular usage, which refers only to infant baptisms, rather reinforces this unhelpful dichotomy.

Those who hold that only believers' baptism is true baptism have, necessarily, to deny that infant baptism is baptism at all, though it leaves them in the rather strange position of having to say that only a tiny minority of Christians throughout the ages have actually been baptized! No doubt the pastor of the Living Stones Church took that view and so, from his perspective,

Philip had *not* been previously baptized. If, however, we take the view that when baptism is conferred on young children it is true baptism, then some very serious issues arise. When Colin and Susan Fox took the decision to have Philip baptized as an infant, it was because they firmly believed infant baptism to be true baptism. From their perspective Philip was already properly baptized. That is why they were so horrified when Philip announced his decision.

This is a situation where the desire to act in a pastorally helpful way comes into sharp conflict with theological and spiritual integrity. It is tempting to respond positively to a request for rebaptism because the person who is making it is so obviously sincere and deeply desires the ceremony. It may be that they have come to a fresh experience of God's love in their own lives, and see being baptized as a believer as a helpful, and biblical, means of testifying to this fact. Or they may say that at their infant baptism they were unable to respond to what was taking place, whereas now they have a personal relationship with Christ and can bring their personal faith to the act of baptism. Sincere and moving though these arguments may be, they run up against the simple fact that baptism is *by nature* unrepeatable. A 'second baptism' is both theological and logical nonsense.

The reason for this lies in the understanding of the nature of baptism which we looked at earlier. Baptism unites us with Christ in his death and resurrection. When we are baptized we belong to Christ, we have entered a new order. We are also initiated into the body of Christ, which is the church. By definition, we cannot be initiated twice. It is a logical impossibility. To be initiated means to enter something (in this case the Christian life) for the first time. When that has taken place, it can never be done again. We can no more be baptized twice than we can be circumcised twice. Because baptism is first and foremost about God's action in our lives, to attempt to repeat it would be to tell God that his first attempt was not

44

good enough. As we have seen, when we baptize young children we declare that God's grace in Christ comes first and we (usually meaning parents and congregation) pledge ourselves to work and pray for the response to come as the child grows up. It might reasonably be said of Philip that this is exactly what happened. Through the loving care of Christian parents he came to the point where the faith in which he had been baptized became personally meaningful for him.

If then we hold to the view that infant baptism is full and valid Christian baptism (and this has been the position of the mainstream church throughout Christian history), we cannot agree to a second ceremony which would, in effect, make a mockery of that infant baptism. Indeed, we might ask what such a 'rebaptism' actually is. If baptism is actually unrepeatable, it follows that 'rebaptism' is not baptism at all. At best it is a ceremony which purports to be baptism.

Dealing pastorally with the needs of Philip and others like him and, at the same time, holding to the integrity of the baptism which has already been given is not an easy task. It would be important to find out what Philip feels is missing from his Christian experience and witness because he was baptized in infancy, and to see if there is some way in which those needs could be met. If he has not been confirmed, then the Confirmation Service offers an opportunity for him to publicly claim for himself what was conferred on him in his baptism. If he feels the need to make a personal testimony to what Christ has now done in his life, opportunity could be created for this testimony to be given in public worship. Or it may be appropriate for there to be a service including the renewal of baptismal promises. There is a good example of such a service in the Anglican *Alternative Service Book 1980* where one of the prayers includes the petition: 'Keep us faithful to our baptism, and so make us ready for that day when the whole creation shall be made perfect in your Son, our Saviour Jesus Christ.'

Sometimes there can be genuine doubt about whether or not a person has been baptized, as in the case of someone from a non-churchgoing family coming to personal faith in mid-life, whose parents are no longer alive to testify and where no baptismal certificate exists. In that situation the universal practice of the church is to administer baptism using the following words: '*N.*, if you are not already baptized, I baptize you in the Name of the Father, and of the Son, and of the Holy Spirit.' This procedure recognizes that God alone knows the real facts and the situation can be left to him to sort out!

Philip's decision to be rebaptized raises another controversial issue. In the course of arguing with his father, Philip said, 'I'm going to be baptized properly, by total immersion.' Part of the attraction of rebaptism for Philip, and others like him, is not only that it is a conscious act, undertaken as a believer, but also that the manner in which such a baptism takes place is very different from the way in which infants are often baptized. Baptism by immersion in a large amount of water (whether this is in a baptistry in church, a swimming pool, a river, or the sea) is a very dramatic and powerful act. Some would also argue that it is more in keeping with the biblical imagery about baptism.

A baptism in which the candidate is totally immersed in water may indeed be a moving experience and it can make a powerful impression on those who witness it. The action appears to signify a wholehearted and total involvement of the person who is being baptized, by the side of which putting a small amount of water on a baby's forehead seems like a quite different activity. Nevertheless, it is important to keep a sense of proportion.

It is perfectly true that what we know about Jewish proselyte baptisms suggests that they involved the person being baptized taking a ritual bath. It is also clear that the baptisms performed by John the Baptist took place in the river Jordan. But it does not follow that immersion is the only possible mode of

Christian baptism, or even the preferred one. It is a striking fact that we do not find instruction about the mode of baptism anywhere in the New Testament. Nor does it seem possible to argue that immersion was taken for granted as the normal method of baptism, thus making instruction about it unnecessary. Indeed, some of the baptisms recorded in the Acts of the Apostles would have been difficult or impossible to perform by immersion. For example, Philip baptized the Ethiopian eunuch in a spring in the desert where the quantity of water available would not have been sufficient for immersion to take place (Acts 8.36–40). The New Testament writers were, we may judge, very wise in not insisting on immersion as necessary to baptism. Otherwise, how would we baptize in those many places where water is a very scarce commodity?

As we have seen, the New Testament uses various images to point to the significance of baptism. Prominent amongst these are the images of being *buried with Christ* and being *raised with Christ*. Some have argued that total immersion better reflects these images, particularly as Paul uses them in Romans 6.3–5. In such an understanding, the lowering of the candidate into the water corresponds with being buried with Christ and the raising of the candidate out of the water with being raised with Christ. The difficulty with this is that the significance of baptism is about a spiritual sharing in the death and resurrection of Christ, not a physical one. It may be a mistake to look for any kind of exact correspondence between the manner in which baptism is administered and the spiritual reality which it confers. Nevertheless, the impact which baptism by immersion can make may be readily recognized. Whilst this method is not in any way required, it is certainly possible where practical circumstances permit it. For some, coming to a new faith, it is an important symbol of their wholehearted commitment. The church has always recognized this, and allows baptism by immersion for those who have not been previously baptized.

Philip might have felt differently about the need to be baptized by immersion if he could have been assured that his baptism as an infant had involved an appreciable quantity of water! In those churches which practise infant baptism there is now widespread recognition that the placing of a damp finger on a baby's forehead, whilst technically valid, does not adequately express the New Testament imagery. The great theologian, Karl Barth, perhaps exaggerating to make a point, wrote that baptism should be a 'threat to life'. Most contemporary baptismal liturgies contain an instruction similar to that found in *The Methodist Worship Book*: 'The minister pours water generously and visibly three times on the child's head, or dips the child in water three times . . . ' Whether baptism takes place by immersion, pouring, dipping or sprinkling, it is still baptism, valid and unrepeatable.

For discussion

If after mature consideration Philip decides to go ahead and receive believer's baptism (a) should his parents attend the ceremony, and (b) should he then join the Living Stones Church? What would be the significant factors in deciding these questions?

12

Baptism for the Dead?

Brenda Murray's dilemma is a very real one. Her intellectual understanding is that it would not be right, or indeed possible, to baptize someone after their death. On the other hand, she is a deeply compassionate person, dealing with a young couple whose baby was stillborn and who believe that baptizing him will give him a name and an identity which will be particularly important when the funeral service takes place. Her pastoral instinct is to do whatever the parents will find helpful and she certainly recognizes that a theological discussion about the rights and wrongs of baptizing a stillborn child will not be helpful. As she expresses it: 'My head is telling me one thing, but my heart is telling me something else.'

One of the misunderstandings which has grown up around the baptism of young children is that it is a naming ceremony. This may in part be due to the way in which the infant baptism service in the *Book of Common Prayer* (1662) of the Church of England requires the officiating priest to say to the Godparents immediately prior to the baptism, 'Name this Child.' The same formula is retained in the 1975 *Methodist Service Book*. This is certainly capable of being interpreted to mean that the child is given his or her name in that moment and that this is an essential part of the baptism itself. More recent baptismal liturgies have attempted to avoid this impression. So the Anglican *Alternative Service Book 1980* assumes that the officiating minister has ascertained the child's name before hand, and the rubric immediately prior to the baptism reads: 'He dips *him* in the water or pours water on *him,* addressing *him* by name.' The question is retained in the 1999 *Methodist Worship Book* but in the form, 'What name have you given this child?' which makes it clear that the name has already been given and is not bestowed in baptism.

49

It is easy to see why recent liturgies have taken this approach, but there are other factors which merit consideration. Although the giving of the name is not an essential part of Christian baptism, there is a long association between the two. The fact that in a Christian society (however that is defined) a person's forename is known as the 'Christian' name is evidence of this. Traditionally, those converted to Christianity in non-Christian societies have been given a new, Christian, name at their baptism precisely to mark their new Christian identity (though this practice has been criticized in recent years as being culturally insensitive and it has been abandoned in some places). Many parents feel the need for a ceremony in which a child is given its name, but this need not be a Christian, or even a religious, occasion. Secular naming ceremonies have been available for many years in order to meet the needs of those who deliberately choose not to have their children baptized. It is quite possible that, in Britain in the foreseeable future, some kind of secular naming ceremony will become an option at the Registrar's Office at the point where parents register the birth of their child. So if what was uppermost in Brian and Lorraine's minds was the need for the child to have a name, then there would be no difficulty in Brenda offering a simple naming ceremony which would express God's love for the baby. But what if that suggestion proved insufficient and the parents continued to request baptism? Is Brenda's first reaction – that such a baptism cannot possibly happen – actually correct?

There is a very strange and difficult passage in I Corinthians which, though it does not directly help us with this particular dilemma, may nevertheless offer a different perspective. In I Corinthians 15 Paul is conducting an argument with some of the congregation who, apparently, do not believe in life after death and in particular in the resurrection of the dead. In verses 29–30 he writes: 'Otherwise, what will those people do who receive baptism on behalf of the dead? If the dead are not raised at all, why are people baptized on their behalf?' The practice of being baptized on behalf of the dead is not known anywhere else in the New Testament nor in any orthodox Christian community, and we are at a bit of a loss to know exactly to what it refers. The most likely explanation, amongst the dozens that have been offered, is that some people who were in the process of becoming Christians died before they could be baptized. Christian friends were therefore baptized on their behalf so that they could be thought to be incorporated into the church. Or it might just possibly have been that some believers were undergoing baptism on behalf of dead friends and relations who have never heard the gospel, in the hope of bringing them within the realm of salvation. It is this latter interpretation which is accepted by the Mormons, who still practise such baptisms. All this seems very strange to orthodox Christians today. We do not know how strange it seemed to Paul, who neither condemns nor approves of it, but merely uses the existence of this practice to buttress his arguments in favour of life after death (if life after death does not exist, why do people do this?). Since this passage refers to the living being baptized *on behalf of* the dead, not to the actual baptism of the dead, it does not directly answer Brenda's dilemma. What it does, however, is to remind us that from time to time there may be baptismal practices in the life of the church which, though difficult to justify from strict logic, do not contradict the basic understanding of what baptism is and may therefore be permitted in exceptional circumstances.

Perhaps this pastoral problem may be viewed as one of those occasions. The most important thing must surely be to reassure the bereaved parents of God's love, both for them and for the stillborn child. As we have seen, one important meaning of baptism is that it declares God's love and grace to the one being baptized. When the person being baptized is an infant, this declaration is made before any personal response is possible. In the case of a stillborn child, the parents whose child it is will have known love for that child long before birth. Christians would want to say that God also loves the child in this way. If, as a result of her conversation with Brian and Lorraine, Brenda concludes that baptism is the only thing which will adequately demonstrate God's love for the child, it will be difficult to refuse the baptism, though it should be regarded as exceptional.

For discussion

What alternatives to baptism would you want to explore with the parents, and what decision would you make if, after discussion, they still requested baptism?

Part 2

Holy Communion

13

Why Sacraments At All?

There was an air of slight apprehension amongst some of the housegroup members as they assembled in Julie's home for their regular Tuesday evening meeting. More than one person was wondering whether they had bitten off more than they could chew! It all started at a Church Council the previous week. During 'Any Other Business' Julie, in the friendliest possible way, had thrown down a challenge to Stephen, their minister. 'Stephen,' she had said, 'we now have communion services a lot more often than we used to. Yet I can't remember the last time I heard a sermon about the meaning of Holy Communion, not just from you but from anyone, lay or ordained. Why don't you do something about it?' Quite what Julie expected Stephen to say in reply she was not sure. What she had certainly not expected was that Stephen would, also in the friendliest possible way, throw the challenge back to her. But that is what he did. Having asked the other members of the Church Council whether Julie's view was widely shared, and having noted from a number of nods round the room that it was, he replied: 'That seems like a very good idea and I shall be happy to respond to it. But I want to be sure that I deal with the issues which genuinely interest and concern you, not just the ones I think you *ought* to be interested in! So I suggest that you take this idea back to your housegroup, have a series of discussions about Holy Communion, and then let me have a list of the subjects you would like to hear about. Is that all right?' Julie looked across the room at John and Marian, two other members of the housegroup who were also on the Church Council, and they signalled that it was. So Julie had replied, 'Yes, Stephen, that's fine by us,' and the meeting had moved on to another discussion. But what had seemed a good idea at the time began to feel a bit different by the time the housegroup came round.

55

Would they really want to talk about Holy Communion, and what would they find to say?

In the event Julie need not have worried. It was John who got the discussion going, though not in the way which might have been predicted. 'I want to begin a bit further back than Stephen asked us to,' he said. 'I'd also noticed that we have more communion services than we used to do. What I want to know is, why do we have them at all?' 'I'm not sure I follow what you mean,' said Betty. 'We've always had communion services. I admit they're a bit different these days. When I was young they seemed to be added on to the end of the main service and not everyone stayed for them. But we've always had them.' 'I agree with you,' Alan chimed in. 'Surely Holy Communion is something all Christians do, isn't it? I was always taught that Jesus told his followers to do it in remembrance of him. I don't quite see what you're driving at, John.'

'Sorry,' said John. 'I don't mean to upset anyone, but I wonder what Jesus meant by that. Did he mean there was to be a special service with bread and wine at which his followers should remember him? Or did he mean that whenever they came together, for a meal or anything else, they should remember him?' 'I'd never thought of it like that before,' commented Marian. 'You can't leave it there, John. Tell us more.' So John continued. 'I think you know that I have a Quaker friend,' he said. 'We've had several conversations about what we each believe. He explained to me that the Quakers don't have any sacraments because they don't think they are necessary. They believe the whole of life should be sacramental and that we should be able to find God in everything. I think there might be something in that.'

'I respect that point of view, of course,' responded Tom. 'But I can't agree with it. I have found taking communion a great source of strength when I most needed it. I would miss it terribly if we stopped doing it.' 'So would I,' said Mollie

56

warmly. 'When I receive the bread and wine I remember that Jesus died for me, and I go back to my seat just wanting to praise him for being so wonderful.' 'I think I envy you and Tom,' said Christine. 'I take communion regularly, of course, and occasionally I feel very close to God. But most of the time it doesn't seem to make much difference. And I can feel very close to God through other things too. Does that make me a bit odd?' 'Well,' said Julie, sensing coffee time approaching, 'We've certainly come up with one big question for Stephen: do we need Holy Communion at all?'

Reflections

Archbishop William Temple once described Christianity as 'the most materialistic of the world's great religions'. He meant it as a compliment, not a criticism. Whereas some religious traditions look down on material things, regarding them as either irrelevant or dangerous, Christianity, at least when it has been true to its origins, sees the material world as the good creation of a gracious God. In the first account of creation in Genesis, we are told that God saw everything he had made – including human beings – and that it was very good (Genesis 1.31). That is the point from which we begin. Whatever sin, corruption and decay might follow, the creation never wholly loses its capacity to reflect the goodness of God, nor human beings the image of the One who created them. This means, amongst other things, that we can take delight in other people for who and what they are and we can enjoy the sensual and sensory things of life. They are the good gifts of a loving God and, in a significant sense, point beyond themselves to God who gave them. For material things are not only created by God, they are used by God.

This is what it means to see the whole of life as 'sacramental'. In this respect and to that extent, the Quaker perception is undoubtedly right. Even ordinary everyday things

57

can reveal the presence and the glory of God to us. And they often do! We do not have to be mystics to be deeply moved by beauty or truth and, above all, overwhelmed by love. Sometimes we become consciously aware that such things are more than just gifts of God to us, they are experiences of God's actual presence with us, for it is through *particular* experiences that we are shaped and moulded. Our experience of love is not of something we might call 'love in general'. It is, rather, of being loved by particular people, parents, partners, children, friends. We are moved to rapture and joy not by 'music in general' but by a particular symphony or song, or the sound of a particular voice. And so, although all of life is potentially sacramental, we experience this dimension in focussed ways. These are examples of what we might call God's specific disclosures of himself.

Yet here we need to be careful. The danger of looking for God in all things is that we fail to recognize that there are some things in which God *cannot* be found. The world, human nature included, is also full of difficulty, danger, corruption and evil. There needs to be a process of discernment. We need also to see how God works in the lives of human beings, bringing both judgment and new revelation. In the Hebrew scriptures we have the story of how the Israelites were chosen so that the nation might be a light to other nations. Within Israel, people such as the prophets were chosen in order to disclose more of God's nature and will to those around them.

Christians believe that this principle reached its ultimate goal in the life, death and resurrection of Jesus of Nazareth (though we must be careful here, since Christians also believe that God's disclosure in Jesus was in some way different in kind as well as in degree). Hebrews 1.3 captures this in an audacious image: 'He is the reflection of God's glory and the exact imprint of God's very being.' Although the image of God is present in every human being, and every person is thus potentially capable of disclosing something of God to us, only in *this* human being is that image so complete that he is the exact imprint of God's very being. Again, the Prologue to John's Gospel, marvelling at the incarnation, says: 'And the Word became flesh and lived among us.' We note how carefully John chooses the word 'flesh'. We are not to be allowed to think that God has appeared on earth as a sort of pretend human being. The Word actually *becomes* flesh in John's account - so there is no looking down on matter here!

The principle which underlies the Christian sacraments is that God takes material things and uses them as vehicles of his love and presence. In the case of Holy Communion those material things are bread and wine. Charles Wesley describes them as:

> Fit channels to convey thy love
> To every faithful heart (*Hymns and Psalms* 602, v.2).

It is not that we cannot find God anywhere else, but that we can always find him here. The sacraments are the focus for the sacramentality of the whole of life. The Quaker protest is against trying to *confine* God's presence to the sacraments. It is a proper one but it goes too far. As somebody once put it: 'We will not find God in the general unless we first find him in the particular,' and the sacraments are the particular means by which God chooses to offer human beings his love and grace. This is not to say that every time we share in Holy Communion, for example, we shall necessarily be conscious of God's presence with us; that point was properly made by Christine. But here we may know that love is being offered to us and, when we share in that action in faith, that love becomes ours.

For discussion

In what ways do you think the bread and wine of Holy Communion may themselves help us to understand all of life as sacramental?

14

Last Supper and Lord's Supper

The second meeting of the housegroup was at Mollie's house and it got off to a flying start. Almost before the last person to arrive had got her coat off Marian said, 'I've been thinking all week about what John said last time. You remember: whether or not Jesus intended us to have a special service with bread and wine. I'm sure he did, because he said 'Do this in remembrance of me.' But what I've been pondering is why our communion services are so very different from the Last Supper as we read about it in the Gospels. Surely when he said, 'Do this', Jesus intended us to re-enact what took place then!' 'Different in what ways?' asked Tom. 'I think they're pretty similar in most respects. After all, the minister always says the words which Jesus said about the bread being his body and the wine his blood.' 'Yes, but I know what Marian means,' Christine interjected. 'So far as we can tell the Last Supper was a very simple occasion – just Jesus and his friends gathered in an upper room for a meal. But our communion services can be quite elaborate, with hymns and prayers and a sermon. And sometimes we have baptisms and commissionings and other things too. When Stephen comes to our first housegroup meeting each year and leads a communion in one of our houses it's much more informal, much more like I think the Last Supper would have been.'

'I also think the Last Supper would have been a very solemn occasion,' Alan suggested. 'After all, Jesus knew his death was coming very shortly. Yet our communion services aren't particularly solemn; well, they are in one sense, but in another they're not, if you know what I mean.' 'I know just what you mean,' Betty commented. 'I think there's been a change in the last few years. When I was young, and the communion part was added on to the end of the main service, it was much more solemn. We used to sing hymns about the death of Jesus.

Nowadays the atmosphere is much more joyful. There's even been a change in the way we announce the service. When I was young it used to be said that it would be 'administered'; now Stephen talks about it being 'celebrated' and surely that's a joyful word.' 'Oh, but that's much better,' said Julie. 'I think "administered" is awful. It makes it sound like a nasty medicine – or a government office! But I don't think communion services ought to be gloomy.' 'Not gloomy, just more like the Last Supper,' said Alan. 'This may be a naïve question,' said John, 'But if it really is meant to be a re-enactment of the Last Supper, why don't we call it that instead of Holy Communion?'

'It isn't always called that either,' Julie pointed out. 'When my sister got married she became a Catholic like her husband, and they call it Mass.' 'We call it the Lord's Supper as well, don't we?' asked Mollie. 'That's a bit nearer to Last Supper, though it's not quite the same.' Betty said, 'Yes, and in my youth it was usually referred to as simply as 'the sacrament'. Even then I thought that was silly because there's more than one!' 'Years ago, before we moved here, we had some friends who went to a little independent chapel, and they used to call it 'The Breaking of Bread,' said Christine. 'I didn't really understand why anyone should call it that because our bread was already cut up into tiny cubes. But when we started using the newer services abut twenty-five years ago, we started to break the bread in the service as well. So it's all the same thing really, isn't it?' 'That was what Sandra used to say when she was our minister. She always referred to it as the Eucharist,' said Tom. 'She said it was a word which could be used by all the different denominations and that was a good thing.' 'Well, anything which helps to break down the barriers between our churches is to be welcomed, and it's certainly a pity if the title we use creates misunderstandings,' Marian commented.

'I don't suppose it really matters what we call it,' suggested Christine. 'What is important is that we meet together, just as the disciples did at the Last Supper, and we eat bread and drink wine in memory of Jesus. That's all there is to it, surely?' 'Well, there's been quite a lot in tonight's discussion for us to pass on to Stephen,' said Mollie. And with that it was time for coffee.

Reflections

It is true that Holy Communion services are not a simple re-enactment of the Last Supper Jesus shared with his disciples. Marian was right to point that out. But they are not intended to be, and to understand the reasons for that we must put the Last Supper in the context of other things in the Gospels which have influenced the church's understanding.

During his earthly ministry, particularly as it is depicted in Luke's Gospel, Jesus frequently shared meals, not only with his regular group of disciples, but with leading people in the community (Luke 7.36–50; 14.1), with those he called to follow him (Luke 8.27–35) and with social outcasts as a sign of acceptance (Luke 19.1–10). He used the images of feasting to indicate the nature of kingdom of God (Matthew 8.11; Luke 13.29) and to express joy over the repentance of a sinner (Luke 15.23–24). Holy Communion must be set within this pattern of sharing and teaching.

The Last Supper itself was probably a Jewish Passover meal, though some scholars think it was more akin to a kind of fellowship meal which Jewish rabbis held with their followers. In either event Jesus acted as the host – the head of the household, if it was a Passover meal. The Gospel accounts of the meal do not tally in precise detail (as we see if we compare Mark 14.17–31 with Matthew 26.20–30 and Luke 22.14–23) but they agree in broad outline about what happened. At some point during the meal Jesus took bread, offered a prayer of thanks over it, broke it into pieces and gave it to the disciples with the words, 'This is my body.' At another point during the meal he took a cup of wine and gave it to his disciples with the words, 'This is my blood of the covenant.' Only in Luke do the words, 'Do this in remembrance of me,' appear.

However, the earliest account of the Last Supper which we possess comes from Paul, writing in I Corinthians 11.23–26. Although very few New Testament documents can be dated with absolute precision, there is widespread agreement that I Corinthians dates from about AD 55–57. We shall need to come back to it in a different way later, but for the moment we note that Paul's account agrees with the essential elements in the Synoptic Gospels, but adds the words 'Do this in remembrance of me' to Jesus' words over the bread as well as the wine. Although the Last Supper is related primarily to the forthcoming death of Jesus, it is not a funeral tea! In all the Gospel accounts there is a looking forward to what lies beyond death, significantly described by Jesus as drinking new wine with them in the kingdom of God.

After the resurrection the Gospels record shared meals with the risen Lord and the disciples. In John 21.4–14 Jesus shares breakfast with them. In Luke 24.41–43 he is reported as eating in their presence. There may have been other, unrecorded occasions, for it is very interesting that, when Peter explained to Cornelius how the risen Lord made himself known, he described the disciples as 'those who ate and drank with him after he rose from the dead' (Acts 10.41). The table fellowship of Jesus and his followers continued after the resurrection.

But the most significant story is of Jesus appearing to two people as they returned to Emmaus following the crucifixion (Luke 24.13–35). This is a table fellowship to which they invite him, though they do not yet know who he is. The crucial act of recognition came, at table, when the risen Christ took bread, offered a prayer of thanks over it, broke it into pieces and gave it to them – precisely the actions which all the accounts give of what Jesus did at the Last Supper. It is in that moment that they recognize him and, as they do so, he vanishes. They return to

Jerusalem bursting with their news and, when they tell the disciples gathered there, what has happened is described as 'how he had been made known to them in the breaking of the bread'. The Emmaus meal is therefore the first time that Jesus is recognized as the Messiah who was crucified, but who is now risen. It is the first meal of the new age – the age of the resurrection. We may say that the Emmaus meal shows the transition between the Last Supper and the Lord's Supper.

This is why the sacrament of Holy Communion is not and ought not to be a precise re-enactment of the Last Supper. That was a once for all historical event. Its meaning and significance look forward to what Jesus was to accomplish on the cross, but beyond that to the new wine of the kingdom of God and the age of resurrection. When Christians gather together to share table-fellowship with Jesus, as it were, it is not with a Master who is about to die, but with a Lord who has risen from death. And so the task of remembering Jesus as we share in bread and wine is far more than recalling his physical sufferings and death, real though those were. It is about acknowledging, gladly and gratefully, everything his death won for us in terms of freedom from sin's dominion, and rejoicing that we recognize his risen presence in the breaking of the bread. It is because our sacramental meals take place *this* side of the resurrection that they are celebrations of the Lord's Supper, not repetitions of the Last Supper.

At one point one of the housegroup members wondered whether Jesus had intended to institute a special meal, or had simply wanted his followers to remember him every time they came together, for a meal or anything else. The two possibilities are not mutually exclusive, of course; the question is whether Jesus intended a special act of remembrance. The universal tradition of the church is that he did. As we have seen, Paul gives us the earliest account of the Last Supper, and he does so in the context of the church's worship practice. He is not relaying a piece of historical information for its own sake;

he is referring to it so that their somewhat chaotic worship life may be put right. Paul introduces his account with the words: 'For I received from the Lord what I also handed on to you . . .' (I Corinthians 11.23). There are two significant things to note about this phrase. In the first place, Paul is not about to tell the Corinthian Christians anything they do not already know. Rather, he is reminding them of something he has already taught them. So the Corinthian church was taught to celebrate the Lord's Supper right from the beginning. In the second place, what Paul is writing about is not something he has thought up for himself; he has received it from the Lord. We cannot be sure whether this means he received it in a direct revelation from the risen Christ or, perhaps more probably, that this is a way of saying that, even though he has been taught it by other people (presumably the disciples who were there), it is not their invention either but goes back to Christ himself. In any event he has not merely taught them about it, but has 'handed it on' to them – a technical phrase for passing on a received tradition. Quite certainly Paul believed that Christ had instituted this rite and, if those who were there had taught him about it, so did they.

References to the celebration of Holy Communion elsewhere in the New Testament are rare, presumably because, as with baptism, it was very much a normal part of congregational life. Acts 2.42 and 20.11 seem to suggest this and in both those references it is called by what is probably its earliest (possibly Palestinian) name, 'the breaking of bread'.

The names by which this sacrament has been called caused some confusion amongst members of the housegroup, as well they might. Most of them carry what we might call historical baggage with them. That is to say, they have been used to describe this sacrament within different parts of the church which differ in their understanding of what it means. Thus a Baptist would never refer to it as the Mass nor a Roman Catholic as the Breaking of Bread. Perhaps in an ecumenical age we can learn to value the particular meanings which lie behind each title.

1. *Mass*. This is the name which is generally, though not invariably, used in the Roman Catholic church. Nobody seems absolutely certain how this term arose, though several ingenious suggestions have been made. The most likely is that it derives from the Latin words *Ite: missa est* ('Go: the congregation is dismissed') used when those who were in training for membership of the church were required to leave. It is difficult to find any spiritual significance in it.

2. *Holy Communion*. Originally the term 'communion' referred only to the moment of taking the elements of bread and wine. After the Reformation, particularly in England, it began to be used for the entire service. It has the merit of reminding us that when we share in the elements we really are sharing in the new life Christ came to bring us. Its disadvantage, perhaps, is that it can seem rather individualistic, as if 'making my communion' is the most important thing. Amongst major denominations Anglicans and Methodists would be most likely to use this term.

3. *Lord's Supper*. This, as we have seen, is the title which Paul uses. It became popular again after the Reformation and was used in the Anglican Prayer Book of 1549, but not in 1662. It would most likely find favour today amongst Baptists, Methodists and members of the URC. It has the merit of pointing to its biblical origins. Some people feel that to celebrate any kind of supper at 10.30 a.m. is an odd thing to do.

4. *Breaking of Bread*. This, as we have noted, is the earliest known name for this sacrament and appears several times in the Acts of the Apostles. It refers to one of the four actions which Jesus did at the Last Supper and in I Corinthians 10.16–17 Paul draws out its theological significance. The one bread, which has to be broken before it is shared, witnesses to the oneness of the church in Christ. The weakness of this title is that it really needs to be explained before it can be understood. It is used by

some Independent and House Churches and among Brethren congregations.

5. *Eucharist.* This term comes from the Greek word *eucharistia* which means 'thanksgiving' and thus refers to another of the four actions which Jesus did at the last Supper. It emphasizes the fact that the Thanksgiving is the central prayer of the service. Although the title has been used to describe this sacrament from the beginning of the second century, it has never really been a 'party' word, associated with any one denomination or tradition. In recent years it has been revived, with some success, first amongst biblical scholars and theologians who find it a usefully 'neutral' word, but also amongst clergy and lay people across a wide range of denominations.

For discussion

Which name, or names, for this sacrament do you find most helpful? What important aspects of its meaning are brought out by the names which other Christians use?

15

What Happens at Communion?

At the end of the previous week's meeting Christine suggested that what we are doing when we celebrate the Eucharist is to eat bread and drink wine in memory of Jesus. At the housegroup's third meeting they explored this idea in more depth. It was Julie who began. 'After last week's meeting,' she said, 'I was telling my sister – the one who became a Catholic when she got married – what we had been talking about. She said this is one of the big differences between Catholics and Protestants. Catholics believe that when the priest says the same words as Jesus said, the bread and wine actually *become* the body and blood of Christ, though they still look the same. That's why Catholics treat the bread and wine with great reverence. When the priest lifts up the consecrated bread they kneel in worship. I'm not sure I understood everything she said, but it was very interesting. She wrote out a verse from a hymn they sometimes sing at her church. I'll read it to you. This is how it goes:

> O bread of heaven, beneath this veil
> thou dost my very God conceal;
> my Jesus, dearest treasure, hail;
> I love thee and adoring kneel;
> each loving soul by thee is fed
> with thine own self in form of bread.'
> (*Celebration Hymnal*, 213, v. 1)

There was a pause whilst the housegroup members thought about this, and then Marian said, 'That's not so very different from some of the hymns we sing. What about that lovely little hymn by Charles Wesley, 'Jesus, we thus obey'? If I remember rightly there's a verse in that which runs:

He bids us drink and eat
Imperishable food;
He gives his flesh to be our meat,
And bids us drink his blood.'
(*Hymns and Psalms*, 614, v.5)

'Oh Marian, I wish I could remember hymns like you do!'
said Tom. 'And that's one of my favourites too. But I don't
think it's saying quite the same thing as the one Julie read to us,
though I can't say why.' 'To be honest,' John commented, 'I've
always found that language about eating the body of Christ and
drinking his blood rather difficult. It sounds a bit cannibalistic
somehow. I know it's really symbolic language, but I'm not
very comfortable with it. For instance, when the minister puts
the cup into my hands and says, 'The blood of Christ, shed for
you.' I would prefer it to be, 'This represents the blood of
Christ, shed for you.' Am I the only one who feels like that?' 'I
don't mind that language at all,' said Mollie. 'In fact it helps
me to feel closer to Jesus and to love and praise him more.
After all, we don't believe anything actually happens to the
bread and wine, do we? Surely they are just symbols of Jesus?
There isn't anything sacred about the bread and wine
themselves, is there? I know for a positive fact that Mrs
Benson, our Communion Steward, puts any left-over bread out
for the birds.' 'I don't feel altogether happy about that,' said
Julie. 'I don't mean that I believe what my sister believes, but if
the minister has spoken the words of Jesus over the bread and
wine, and we have used them in such a special way, surely we
ought to be a bit more reverent than that!' 'What really matters,
in my view,' said Alan, 'is our own faith. In one of the
invitations to communion we are invited to 'feed on him in
your hearts by faith with thanksgiving' and I find that a very
helpful thought. I couldn't believe that the bread and wine
actually change into the body and blood of Christ, that sounds
like nonsense to me. But I do believe that, when I receive them

69

in faith, I am fed by Christ. It is our own faith which is important. If somebody received communion without believing in Jesus, they wouldn't receive anything at all – except bread and wine, of course.' The housegroup members pondered this for a while. It came close to saying what many of them really felt, though perhaps in slightly different ways. But Christine wasn't sure that she entirely agreed with her husband. 'You put that beautifully Alan,' she said. 'But it is a bit too sophisticated for me; I'm a simple soul, really. I just think that when we take bread and wine in memory of Jesus, we feel closer to him. I'm not sure it helps to talk about being fed, or about receiving something. We just remember Jesus and what he did for us.' 'Is remembering always a simple thing?' asked Betty. 'It seems to me that, when I remember our Paul, it's a bit like actually bringing him back, as if he were really with us. I know he isn't because he died nearly twenty years ago, but it feels like it. I'm not quite sure how to put this, but I'll have a go! If remembering someone who is dead can be as vivid and real as that, surely remembering Jesus, who we believe is alive again, must be like making him really present, mustn't it?'

Reflections

The housegroup discussion ranged over deep and important theological questions, but also to some extent, over ancient controversies in the life of the church, some of which, because we think of the world somewhat differently, are no longer as relevant to us today as once they were. There are two major issues, which in their traditional expression may be broadly summarized as follows. The first is this: is there a 'Real Presence' of the risen Christ in the Eucharist, in some way connected with the consecrated bread and wine? The second is this: if there is such a 'Real Presence' of the risen Christ in the Eucharist, does this involve some kind of change in the elements themselves?

We can begin with Julie's summary of what Catholic Christians have traditionally believed. She said, 'Catholics believe that when the priest says the same words as Jesus said, the bread and wine actually *become* the body and blood of Christ, though they still look the same.' This doctrine is usually known as *transubstantiation*. It is an extraordinarily subtle teaching and almost any summary will do it less than justice. It begins from the view held by philosophers in the ancient world that any material object (not just bread or wine) possesses (a) a substantial reality or 'substance' which is what it *really* is, and (b) 'accidents', which are the characteristics of what we *perceive* it to be. From this starting point, the doctrine of transubstantiation states that, when the bread and wine are consecrated the 'substance' is changed into the body and blood of Christ, whilst the 'accidents' still remain those of bread and wine. In other words, though invisible to the senses, the real being of consecrated bread and wine is the body and blood of Christ. One of the major difficulties in holding to this teaching today (and it is one which is freely admitted by many Catholic teachers) is that we no longer think of material things having a 'substance' which is capable of being changed into something else. Bread is what it appears to be – bread; just as wood is what it appears to be – wood, and nothing else. But the value of the doctrine is that it makes the 'Real Presence' of the living Christ objective. Christ has promised to be with his people in this way, and we can be sure that he is. Sometimes the accusation has been levelled that this reduces the Eucharist to a bit of magic, like a conjuring trick, and it cannot be denied that sometimes those who hold to this understanding have treated the consecrated bread and wine in a manner which suggests this. But at its best the doctrine also teaches that, however objective Christ's presence may be, we must still receive in faith in order to receive any benefit.

Transubstantiation was never the only way of describing how the bread and wine become the vehicles for Christ's 'Real

Presence'. Another is sometimes called *consubstantiation* and this was favoured by the great German Reformer Martin Luther. He described Christ's body and blood as existing in the bread and wine in much the same way as fire exists in a piece of iron when it has been heated.

Others have attempted to safeguard the 'Real Presence' whilst denying that there is any actual change in the bread and wine at all. In former times people who held this view were described as 'Virtualists'. In more recent times the term 'Transignification' has been used. That word tells us that we are looking not at a change in the reality of the bread and wine, but a change in their *significance*. This seemed to be what Julie was driving at when she said that, if the minister has spoken the words of Jesus over the bread and wine and we have used them in such a special way, they ought to be treated with reverence. A number of illustrations have been offered to explain this way of understanding the Eucharist.

A goldsmith takes a piece of gold and makes two wedding rings from it. They are both still pieces of gold, nothing more or less. Then a couple buy them for their forthcoming wedding. In the marriage service they each put a ring on the other's finger as a sign of their marriage, and the action is accompanied by a promise. What are those rings then? Well, they are both still pieces of gold, exactly the same as they were before. They have not changed but, because of what has happened, what they mean and signify has. Now they signify the love and trust that the marriage celebrates. Either partner, looking at the ring on his or her finger, will remember that he or she is married, and to whom. If one of those rings should be lost, more than a piece of gold will have been lost and it cannot be easily replaced by going and buying another. The gold used to make the ring has not changed, but it is not in all respects the same as it was before the wedding. In the same way the bread and wine of the Eucharist does not change, but it is not the same as it was before it was taken and set apart for a holy use. It now conveys Christ's presence to us.

Others would deny any doctrine of the Real Presence at all. Like Christine and Mollie, they would say that there is no 'objective' presence. The presence of the risen Christ is in the hearts and minds of those who come to worship, not in the bread and wine at all. We use bread and wine because that is what Jesus told us to do, and as we receive them in faith, we remember Jesus who is present within us and our faith is strengthened. This view is sometimes known as 'Receptionism'. Those who hold it have sometimes been accused of believing in the 'Real Absence', but that is unfair, because they would certainly want to insist that the Risen Presence of Christ is in the believer's soul and life. The obvious attraction of this view is that it appears to avoid some of the rather sterile controversies of the past and not (as we might think is the case with some other views) claim to know more than we really can. Its weakness is that it does not really take with sufficient seriousness the conviction, which runs throughout church history from the earliest times onwards, that when we share in the bread and wine we really are sharing in a relationship with Christ. Paul certainly seems to think this, when he writes: 'The cup of blessing that we bless, is it not a sharing in the blood of Christ? The bread that we break, is it not a sharing in the body of Christ?' (I Corinthians 10.16). These are rhetorical questions. Paul is not expecting his readers to search for an answer; they know that the answer is 'yes' because that is what they have been taught. Of course, neither here nor anywhere else does the New Testament say anything about the *manner* of Christ's real presence, but Paul certainly appears to be affirming that, when we share communion, we do more than simply hold a memorial meal for Jesus.

We might also pause on what Betty said about the meaning of 'remembering'. As she said, we are not just recalling an absent figure. It is much more like making someone present with us now. Much biblical scholarship would support that view, and many would argue that, when in our worship we remember what God has done for us, we in effect re-call that event into the present so that it becomes effective again for us. If this is true, it will have an important influence on what we believe we are doing when we 'remember' Jesus with bread and wine, this side of the resurrection.

At the beginning of this Reflection I suggested that some of these issues are ancient controversies which are no longer relevant to us in the way they once were. But we might remember that at some periods of the church's history, when interest in theological questions was more intense than it is now, people's view of what actually happened (or did not happen) in the Eucharist could be literally a matter of life or death for them. There is a famous verse, said to have been spoken by the politically shrewd Queen Elizabeth I when asked her view of the matter. It runs:

> Christ was the Word that spake it;
> He took the bread and brake it;
> And what that word doth make it,
> That I believe, and take it.

There are many in today's church who would be quite happy with so evasive an answer. Does that simply mean that we have become intellectually flabby? Or is there an important point to recognize here, namely that when we have done our thinking to the best of our ability, we have to acknowledge that the presence of Christ in the Eucharist is one of God's great mysteries? It may be that we have to receive it with gratitude rather than imagine that we could ever solve it. John and Charles Wesley wrote an entire hymn about the impossibility of ever knowing the answer. It begins:

74

> O the depth of love divine,
> The unfathomable grace!
> Who shall say how bread and wine
> God into man conveys?

and finishes:

> Sure and Real is the grace,
> The manner be unknown;
> Only meet us in thy ways,
> And perfect us in one.
> Let us taste the heavenly powers;
> Lord, we ask for nothing more:
> Thine to bless, 'tis only ours
> To wonder and adore.
>
> (*Hymns on the Lord's Supper 1745:* no. 57)

For discussion

Which view of the presence of Christ in Holy Communion do you find most helpful, and why? Should the fact that Christians take differing views prevent them from sharing in Holy Communion together?

16

A Common Communion?

'Do you remember,' said Betty at the start of the housegroup's next meeting, 'When we all went to Mass at St Urban's during the Week of Prayer for Christian Unity earlier this year?' 'Yes, I wasn't sure at first that I wanted to go,' said Mollie, 'But afterwards I was glad that I did. Why are you mentioning that?' 'Well,' said Betty, 'One of the things that struck me was how similar the service was to one of our own communion services.' 'I agree with you, it was,' Alan retorted, 'and I'm not sure that's a good thing. I don't want us to become the same as everybody else.' 'Oh, but it's not as if we were becoming like *them* surely,' Marian responded. 'The Catholic Church has changed just as much as we have, if not more. After all, at one time the Mass used to be in Latin!' 'What struck you in particular, Betty?' enquired John, genuinely interested. 'I sort of felt I knew where I was in the service,' said Betty, 'even though many of the words were unfamiliar to me.' 'They weren't all unfamiliar though, not by a long chalk,' Tom interrupted his wife. 'We could have joined in several bits without looking at the book at all.' 'That's true,' said Betty, and continued: 'But even when we couldn't, the service had the same kind of shape as ours. First we had some prayers, then the readings and the sermon, and then exchanged the Peace, just as we do.' 'St Urban's made ever so much more of the Peace than we do, though,' Mollie commented. 'Sometimes at our church the minister says something to us and we make a response, and that's it! I thought it was lovely at St Urban's. I think everyone went and exchanged the Peace with everyone else. Even though it was a strange church to me, I felt really welcomed and I just wanted to praise the Lord for all the fellowship.'

'I agree with you, Mollie,' said Christine, 'though I don't know that I'd want to do it like that every time. But then, the Peace is fairly new to us as well, isn't it? We never used to have it at all.' 'But it was after the Peace that I felt on most familiar ground,' said Betty. 'When we came to the communion itself I expected it to be very different indeed, being in a Catholic church. But the long prayer – the Thanksgiving I think it's called – sounded so much like ours. It even began with the words, 'The Lord be with you' and that was a real surprise I can tell you!' 'There were some differences as well,' Alan interjected. 'I seem to remember some references to Mary and the saints that I wouldn't expect to find in one of our prayers.' 'True, but Betty's right,' said Marian. 'We were all able to join in that bit which begins, 'Holy, holy, holy,' and the priest read the story of the Last Supper, just like we do.'

'It isn't just the Catholics though, is it?' Tom said. 'I think I'm right in saying that the Church of England service is a lot like ours these days. Do you think the high-ups in all the churches have got together and agreed on what to put in the communion service?' 'I suppose they could have done,' said Christine. 'But now I come to think of it, I went to a communion service a few years back where they didn't use a book at all. Do you remember it, Alan? We were on holiday in Devon.' 'Yes,' Alan responded. 'I do. I can't remember now whether it was a Baptist or a Congregationalist church, but I remember going. I very much enjoyed it. Refreshing, I thought, to have a service without a book.' 'Yes, it was good,' Christine agreed. 'But what has suddenly struck me about it, thinking back, is that when the minister – he was quite a young man as I recall – came to the thanksgiving over the bread and wine, although he was praying in his own words, the prayer had much the same shape and said much the same things as the ones we are familiar with. Isn't that interesting?' 'There was one difference now I come to think about it,' mused Alan. 'We usually include the words about the Last Supper inside the prayer, but he read them from the Bible first. I do remember that quite clearly.'

'Fascinating,' said John. 'But what are we going to ask Stephen out of tonight's discussion?'

Reflections

Betty was certainly right to spot that there is now substantial agreement across the churches concerning both the shape of a Eucharist and, in particular, what ought to be included in the Prayer of Thanksgiving which is at its heart. Tom was not as far off the mark as he might have thought, with his suggestion that people might have 'got together' to agree on what ought to be in a communion service, though the matter is rather more complicated than that!

For around a hundred years, scholars whose field of work is Christian worship have been sharing the results of their study and reflection with one another, right across the denominational boundaries. Particularly since the middle of the twentieth century, considerable attention has been given to the origins of Christian worship in the New Testament and its development in the life of the early church (some of those studies have informed the Reflections in this book!). Gradually, the results of these studies and researches have influenced how *all* our churches have thought about worship, both its meaning and content. For example, one result of the scholarly study has been to claim that the Eucharist is central to the worshipping life of the church. As Julie observed in the Church Council which preceded the housegroup discussions, 'We now have communion services a lot more often than we used to.'

In England this process began in the 1950s with the work of the 'Parish and People' movement, and its influence has spread to all the mainstream churches. Another powerful influence was the creation of the Church of South India in 1947. This church brought together Anglicans and Methodists, together with former Congregationalists and Presbyterians (who had already united) and the Basel Mission Church, which stemmed

78

from the European Reformed tradition. Clearly one of the prime requirements of the new church was a new liturgy! In order to create it, the traditions of the uniting churches were not only brought together but, more significantly, were measured against what scholars were uncovering as the tradition of the scriptures and of the early church. The result was a new (and at the time very exciting) communion order which set the pattern for other churches all round the world revising their worship. There is now broad ecumenical agreement on many things (though not all) and the fruit of this continues to be seen in denominational service books. The fact that Alan and Christine were able to attend a service which was conducted entirely without a book, yet where the shape of the service and the contents of the Thanksgiving were still recognizably the same, is a tribute to those who had taught the minister concerned, who was evidently a very well-informed young man! At the same time, he was someone who valued his own tradition, for the unusual feature which Alan remembered – reading the narrative of the Last Supper from the Bible before the prayer began – has long been a feature of eucharistic worship in the Reformed tradition to which both Baptist and Congregationalist churches belong.

So far as the shape of the service is concerned, the housegroup had already spotted what this normally is. The Ministry of the Word, in which the scriptures are read and expounded, is followed by the Lord's Supper, in which the Eucharist is celebrated. It is normally the Peace which leads out of one and into the other. So far as the shape of the Lord's Supper is concerned, the tradition of the church is to follow a four-fold pattern which includes the seven actions Jesus performed with the bread and wine at the Last Supper. These are:

1. *Taking*, where the bread and wine are brought to the Lord's table or uncovered if they are already there, and prepared for use;

2. *Giving Thanks*, which is done in a prayer of thanksgiving;

3. *Breaking,* where the bread is broken in silence or accompanied by words;

4. *Sharing,* which is when the communicants receive the elements.

It is the second of these, the Thanksgiving, which needs some further exploration.

When Jesus gave thanks over the bread and wine at the Last Supper, he would almost certainly have used prayers from the Jewish tradition. A very beautiful one over the bread runs: 'Blessed are you, O Lord our God, King of the universe, for you bring forth bread from the earth.' When Christians give thanks over the bread and wine at the Lord's Supper, we are doing so in the new resurrection age, in which the long story of God's love to us, including the story of Jesus, is the proper subject for all our thanksgiving. Building on the work of those who have studied the earliest liturgies of the church – of which from time to time new examples are still being discovered – there is widespread ecumenical agreement that eucharistic thanksgivings are normally Trinitarian in shape. That is to say, the first part of the prayer gives thanks for the work of God the Father in creating the world and ourselves; the second part of the prayer gives thanks for the work of God the Son in the salvation of the world (usually including the narrative from the Last Supper); and the final part of the prayer gives thanks for the work of God the Holy Spirit, asking that the Spirit may make the things of Christ real to us and enable our act of worship to be fruitful.

So far as the content of the Thanksgiving is concerned, there is again reasonably widespread ecumenical agreement about certain elements which ought normally to be included. However, examination of such prayers, both contemporary and stretching back over the last two thousand years, quickly reveals that there is no agreement on the order in which they should appear, their precise relationship to one another or their wording! With that caution, we may note that they are as follows:

a. *The Introductory Responses.* The familiar form which begins, 'The Lord be with you' said by the presiding minister, comes from the earliest complete text of a eucharistic prayer known to us, dating from AD 215. The whole congregation is invited to join in. It has also been said that this dialogue is the congregation's 'permission' for the minister to proceed with the prayer, since the celebration is the work of the whole people of God gathered in that place.

b. *The Preface.* Here we give thanks to God for his goodness in creation, but most especially for what he has done for us in sending his only Son for the world's salvation.

c. *The Sanctus* (and *Benedictus*). These ancient texts beginning respectively, 'Holy, holy, holy Lord,' and 'Blessed is he who comes . . .' have traditionally been part of the Thanksgiving. The origins of the Sanctus are obscure. The Benedictus comes in part from Mark 11.9 (and parallels) where it greets the coming of Christ into Jerusalem. These texts enable everyone to join in and they lead straight into the next section.

d. *The Institution narrative.* The story of what Jesus did with the bread and wine and the words he said over them is usually placed at this point, though still in the form of prayer ('He gave you thanks . . .'). We are giving thanks not only for what Jesus did at the Last Supper, but also for the whole redeeming work of Christ.

e. *The anamnesis.* This word means 'remembrance'. We are celebrating the Eucharist in fulfilment of Jesus' command to do so in remembrance of him and so in the prayer we specifically mention this. In remembering what Jesus has done we in some sense bring the past into the present, as we have seen. Thus we know that he is with us.

f. *The epiclesis.* This term is used to describe a prayer for the coming of the Holy Spirit, in most traditions on the bread and wine, in others on the worshippers, and in yet others, on both. This is a controversial point. Many modern

81

Thanksgivings have an epiclesis which is deliberately ambiguous, such as: 'Send your Holy Spirit that these gifts of bread and wine . . .' Charles Wesley had no inhibitions. He encouraged us to sing to the Holy Spirit:

> Thy life infuse into the bread,
> Thy power into the wine. (*Hymns and Songs* 602, v. 1)

but not everyone agrees with him!

g. *The oblation.* In Romans 12.1 we are urged to offer ourselves as a living sacrifice to God. Many Thanksgivings include this element, sometimes also offering back to God the bread and wine, which are his gifts to us in the first place.

The Thanksgiving sometimes includes extremely brief intercessions and possibly a prayer that our sharing in communion may be spiritually fruitful. It usually ends with a doxology – words which give all the glory to God, as is right and fitting.

For discussion

Are you happy that the communion orders of the various denominations are much closer to one another than they used to be? What might be the gains and losses in this new situation?

17

The Boundaries of Communion?

When the housegroup assembled for its final meeting, John was very anxious to begin the discussion. 'We spent quite a lot of time last week discussing the Mass we went to at St Urban's, and how like our own service it was,' he said. 'But the more I've thought about it the more I've realized that in two very important respects it wasn't like ours at all.' 'What were those John,' asked Julie. 'Firstly,' John replied, 'when people went up to receive the elements, we weren't allowed to do so. We were told that we could go for a blessing, but we couldn't take communion. That was quite different from our own service, where everyone is welcome, and I didn't like it.' 'That was because we aren't Catholics,' said Christine. 'No, but we're *Christians* aren't we?' said Alan. 'I agree with John. I didn't like that at all. After all, we would have welcomed them to share in communion if the service had been at our church. I don't see what the problem is.' 'And what was the other difference you noticed?' Marian asked John. 'That those who did receive communion only had the bread, and the wine was kept for the priest. That would never happen in our church, would it?' John replied. 'I'm not so sure,' Tom said. 'I heard recently of a Methodist church where the children are given the bread and not the wine.' 'How peculiar,' commented Mollie. 'That's probably in case the children spill the wine on the carpet,' suggested Julie.

'There's something else which has changed quite a lot in recent years,' said Alan, 'Giving children communion. It never used to happen in my young days, and I'm not sure it's right.' 'Oh Alan,' sighed Christine. 'Sometimes you can be terribly set in your ways!' 'Well, I don't like change,' admitted Alan, 'but I think I've got good reason in this case. Some of the children who are given communion are as young as four and five. What can they possibly understand about what they are doing? After all, we've been finding it difficult enough!' 'Yes, but the children are as much part of the church as we are. They've been baptized – well most of them have – and it's very important to make them feel they belong,' Julie replied. 'And after all we don't restrict admission to communion to those who are church members, do we? That's one of the ways in which we differ from the Catholics,' added Betty. Alan could see that he didn't have anybody else's support for his views, so he lapsed into silence. Christine thought she had better change the subject.

'There's one thing I have never really understood,' she said. 'Why is it always the minister who leads the Holy Communion service? Not that I've anything against our ministers, and Stephen is a very fine one. But we have some good lay preachers too, and they never take a communion.' 'I believe it does happen sometimes,' said Tom, 'but I've never experienced it myself.' 'No, and I wouldn't want to!' exclaimed Marian. 'Good gracious, whatever next? My grandmother was Church of England and I used to go regularly with her when I was young. It's always the vicar who takes the service and so it should be. It wouldn't be right for someone who is not ordained to celebrate Holy Communion.' John said, 'But in those days, if you'll forgive me saying so Marian, nobody except the minister did *anything* at communion. Now, lay people read the lessons and quite often the stewards help with the distribution of the bread and wine. Nobody seems to mind that.' 'Actually, I'm not very keen on it,' said Betty. 'I prefer to receive the elements from the minister. But in any case that's quite different from leading the service. I agree with Marian, that wouldn't be right at all.' 'But why should being ordained matter?' asked Mollie. 'So far as I am concerned, anyone who is filled with the Holy Spirit is good enough to lead the service. There's no problem at all!' 'How do you decide that someone is filled with the Holy Spirit?' asked Julie. 'Am I, Mollie?' Whilst Mollie thought about Julie's question, Tom said, 'I don't think leading a communion service is about being good enough. I don't think anybody is good enough to do that. I think it's about who has been called by God and authorized by the church – and I don't mean the local church, I mean the wider church. Stephen has and I haven't. So far as I'm concerned that's all there is to it.'

'I don't mean to be critical,' said John, 'But as I think about our discussions over the past few weeks I fear there has been something rather parochial about some of them. We have sometimes talked as though the Eucharist was a kind of, oh I don't know, club meal, I suppose. That's why I reacted so strongly to some people not being admitted to the table at St Urban's. I know it's a Christian sacrament, celebrated by the church, but I have a feeling it's not just about us, it's about the wider world and its needs. What does the Eucharist have to do with a world full of hungry people, lonely people and victims of injustice? Isn't that worth considering as well?' Everyone else felt a little humbled by John's passion, and by the recognition that he was right. After a silence Julie said: 'I suppose that's something to do with the other meaning of "the body of Christ" – truly being the church. We must certainly ask Stephen to preach about that.'

Reflections

There were four major areas of concern raised in the housegroup discussion, though some of them are linked.

1. *Intercommunion.*

John in particular objected to not being allowed to receive communion in a church of another denomination. When it was pointed out that this was because he did not belong to that denomination, Alan countered this by pointing out that we are all Christians, and surely that was enough. There is, sadly, still a deep division between churches on this issue and it is important to understand the reasons on both sides of the debate.

There are two groups of churches where admission to communion is restricted.

Firstly, for the Roman Catholic and Orthodox churches admission to communion is restricted to those who are said to be 'in communion' with those churches, though Catholics do make some strictly limited exceptions to this. In the case of the Roman Catholic Church, this is partly because it judges that other Christians do not sufficiently agree with them on a number of crucial doctrinal matters, including the nature of the Eucharist, but also because other churches, although they are recognized as possessing 'elements' of the church in all its fullness, do not yet possess that fullness, as Rome believes that it does. For Roman Catholics, therefore, full sharing together in the Eucharist will only become possible when unity has been attained. Intercommunion is seen as the goal of Christian unity, and we have not reached it yet. By the same token, Roman Catholics and Orthodox Christians are not permitted by the rules of their own churches to receive communion in other denominations.

Secondly, a small number of extreme Protestant churches, such as the Strict Baptists, a few Independent churches and House Fellowships, and some minority Presbyterian churches, will not admit anyone to communion except their own members. This is because rigorous spiritual and moral probity is required for admission and they cannot be sure that other people pass those tests. Such an understanding of the nature of the church is probably beyond the reach of argument.

Most mainstream Protestant churches practice an 'open table' policy in varying degrees. The Church of England used to restrict communicant status to those who had been confirmed, but members in good standing from other churches with a Trinitarian understanding of God are now welcomed. Methodism is often said to have an open table practice, and this is undoubtedly true, although it is worth remembering that it is relatively recent! Most mainstream Protestants would argue that intercommunion is not only the goal of Christian unity; it may also be its *means*. This position is grounded in the conviction that the Eucharist is not the possession of any church, but the gift of Christ who is Lord of the church and that we cannot therefore exclude any fellow Christians who belong to Christ through baptism. Indeed, if through the Eucharist we experience the grace and presence of Christ, may not the act of sharing in the Eucharist break down our divisions as we meet Christ together? John Wesley described the Eucharist as a 'converting ordinance' and one of the things from which we may expect it to convert us is our separateness and division.

For discussion

Do you think it is right for Christians to share in communion together before the churches are united? What factors cause you to hold the views you do?

2. *Children at Communion.*

In recent years a number of churches have begun to admit children to communion, not just in the sense of allowing them to be present during the service, but permitting them to receive the bread and wine. For most Protestant churches this has been something of a revolution, though we ought to remember that in the Roman Catholic Church there is a long tradition of children making their 'first communion', usually at about the age of seven, and it has been regarded as a significant occasion. Alan objected to this practice on the grounds that very young children could not understand what they were doing. As he rightly pointed out, the housegroup members had been discussing the meaning of communion for several weeks, and it was not evident that they understood what it meant!

The answer to Alan's problem is, in one sense, to be found in what he said. It is certainly true that young children do not entirely understand what they are doing when they share in the Eucharist. But which of us does? We do not demand of adults that they pass an examination paper in eucharistic theology before they are allowed to participate. Nor would we, for example, exclude mentally handicapped people of any age from participation on the grounds that they were incapable of understanding. The key issue is that anyone who shares in communion should understand what they are doing *at a level which is appropriate to their age and experience.*

Also important is the question of belonging. Once past infancy, even young children know that they belong to the family by sharing in family occasions, including meals. There is no logic by which those who belong to the Christian family through baptism can be excluded from the central activity of that family, which is the Eucharist. There are, of course, some practical questions to be sorted out, but these are never insuperable. Tom mentioned a church where the children were not given the wine. Julie suggested that this was because they might spill it on the carpet. On that basis we should withhold the wine from some older people whose hands are shaky. But we would never think of doing that. We may note in passing John's concern that the wine was withheld from the laity in the service he attended at St Urban's, and he wondered what the reason was. The simple answer is that the church became anxious that, if too many people handled the cup, the wine might be spilt – a particularly difficult thing to cope with you if believe in transubstantiation. There has been widespread recognition in Roman Catholic circles that this practice is difficult to justify, and in many countries the hierarchy has already restored the cup to the laity.

For discussion

Why do you think it is right, or wrong, to admit young children to Holy Communion? If your church already does this, how has it contributed to your understanding of the worship? If your church does not do this, on what basis was that decision taken?

3. *Presidency at the Eucharist.*

Christine asked why it was that communion services were always led by ministers. In the discussion which followed it was clear that there were some strong views on both sides of the argument. We need to make a distinction between sharing the service, and presiding at it. There is no dispute about people who have not been ordained doing a whole range of things within the service including, as was pointed out, assisting with the distribution of the elements. The issue is about presiding at the service. In some traditions the person who does this is called the Celebrant, in others the President or the Presiding Minister.

What does it mean to 'preside' at the Eucharist? Different Christian traditions will answer this in different ways, but most would agree that a minimum definition of presidency is to preside over the four-fold action described in the Reflection in chapter 16. That is to say, the person presiding takes the bread and wine, leads the Thanksgiving, breaks the bread and presides over the sharing of the elements. It is also generally seen as good practice for the presiding minister to begin and end the service and to lead the sharing of the Peace. Who may do these things?

It is important to remember that the Eucharist is never a private occasion: it is always (even when it is a house communion) an act of the church of God. For this reason, the church appoints those who may lead this central act of Christian worship and does not permit this to be done by anyone and everyone. It is true, as is sometimes said, that the New Testament tells us nothing about who should preside at the Eucharist. But it is clear that from the beginning people were appointed to various leadership roles within the church. It is reasonable to assume that presiding over the central act of the church's worship was one of their functions. Appointment was by the 'laying on of hands', which we now call Ordination. Something of what this means can be gleaned from the way in

89

which Timothy was told: 'Do not neglect the gift that is in you, which was given to you through prophecy with the laying on of hands by the council of elders' (I Timothy 4.14).

Whether we agree with it or not, the tradition of the church down the centuries has been that only those who have been ordained may preside at the Eucharist. For those churches which believe that their ordinations may be traced back to the apostles themselves and that they confer a 'priestly' character on the recipient, this is a matter of faith. For them, a Eucharist presided over by someone not properly ordained would not be a Eucharist at all. Most of the churches which stem directly or indirectly from the Protestant Reformation in the sixteenth century do not believe that ordination confers a priestly character. The slogan 'The priesthood of all believers' became popular after the Reformation and is often taken to mean that each individual believer is a priest. As a reminder that every believer has direct access to God, not just through an intermediary, this is both true and welcome, but it does not mean that each and every believer is able to do everything. The New Testament text which bears most directly on this is I Peter 2.9–10, which begins: 'You are a chosen race, a royal priesthood, a holy nation.' As Professor Frances Young has shown, 'This is a corporate not an individual vocation.'

Most Protestant churches do confine presidency at the Eucharist to the ordained, not because the ordained are seen as priests, but because as ordained people they represent and focus the corporate priesthood of the whole church. It is, in many respects, a matter of authority. Who has the authority of the church to exercise the church's corporate priesthood? Those who have been ordained have this authority by virtue of their ordination. Might others who have not been ordained, lay people, be given it too? Mollie was quite happy for anyone who is 'filled with the Holy Spirit' to preside at the Eucharist, but Julie's question shows the difficulty with this position. Who decides whether someone is filled with the Spirit, or spiritually mature, or 'good enough'? And, as Tom pointed out, are those the real issues anyway? Surely the real issue remains one of authority to preside. The issue of extending that authority beyond those who have been ordained has arisen at least twice in our century in schemes of church union. In 1932 the Wesleyan Methodists, the Primitive Methodists and the United Methodists came together to form the Methodist Church. The first of these bodies did not permit lay presidency at the Eucharist, the other two did. In 1972, Congregationalists, who permitted lay presidency at the Eucharist, came together with Presbyterians, who did not, to form the United Reformed Church. In both cases the solution was the same. Lay presidency was permitted, but only in cases of necessity. Presidency by ordained ministers remains the norm. Only where there are insufficient ordained people to meet the need can the norm be breached. If the situation was to be reached where no necessity could be demonstrated, there would be no lay presidency. Also in both cases, proper authorization has to be given by the appropriate church body. This might seem to meet the question of proper authority to which we have referred.

Like most compromises this does not please everybody. Some would argue that there is no theological reason why lay people should not preside on a regular basis and they would like to see the practice widened. Others argue that only ordination can confer the authority to represent the church's corporate priesthood and would therefore wish to see lay authorizations abolished.

For discussion

Would you be happy for the communion services in your church to be presided over by someone who has not been ordained? If so, how should that person be chosen?

4. *A Club Meal?*

John was concerned that the housegroup's discussions about the Eucharist had been rather introverted, giving the impression that the Eucharist was for an 'in' group. He wanted to ask about the relationship of the Eucharist to the world Jesus came to save – and he was right!

The service of Holy Communion for Christmas and Epiphany in the *Methodist Worship Book* has a glorious prayer to be said when the gifts of the people and the bread and wine are brought to the table. It runs:

> Lord and Giver of every good thing,
> we bring to you
> bread and wine for our communion,
> lives and gifts for your kingdom,
> and all for transformation through your grace and love,
> made known in Jesus Christ our Saviour.

What we bring and offer to God, including our souls and bodies, is most woefully inadequate. But God takes and transforms it all by his grace and love, that it may bring blessing and new life to others. The Eucharist is not just an individual act (making my communion), it is the corporate act of the church. As the church is nourished with the body and blood of Christ, so it is formed and shaped to become what it is called to be – the body of Christ in the world. As the body of Christ in the world we are charged with loving others, struggling for justice and bringing peace.

Some of the imagery of the Eucharist reminds us of its wider dimensions. The fact that such ordinary, everyday material objects as bread and wine are at its heart speaks of the importance of those things in the whole of human life. True, human beings do not live by bread alone, but they cannot live *without* bread. How can Christians feed upon the bread of life and not recognize their calling to share bread with others, by giving to aid charities, by supporting fair trade organizations, by campaigning for debt relief and proper overseas aid? The fact that we are all partakers in the one loaf speaks of the importance of unity, the creation of true human community, not just in the church, but outside it too. That sense of community has all but disappeared in our fragmented post-modern world. There are many lonely, frightened, bewildered people in our society. Some of them know for sure that they are not really part of the community. We have told them so very clearly by denying them homes or work and human dignity. The Eucharist holds out the vision of true human community, in which we all share in the one loaf.

If this were a different (and much longer) book, there are many more themes like these which could be explored. One of the joys of eucharistic worship is the way that, as we grow in our understanding of it, we are continually given new insights into the nature of our task as Christian disciples. The Eucharist shapes us into the kinds of Christian communities through which the world is transformed. The Eucharist must never become a private banquet for the select few. It is rather, as Reginald Heber expressed it:

Bread of the world, in mercy broken;
Wine of the soul, in mercy shed. (*Hymns and Psalms*, 599)

For discussion

What connections can you make between the nature of the Eucharist and the concerns of a needy world?

Postscript

This book is called *The Sacraments* and it has dealt with just two sacraments, Baptism and Holy Communion. This would seem very strange to the majority of the world's Christians. Orthodox and Roman Catholics, along with some Anglicans, acknowledge five more sacraments, making seven in all. Some explanation of these seems called for.

1. *Confirmation*

It is difficult, even impossible, to find a biblical basis for confirmation. The practice arose as a consequence of the baptism of young children becoming normative within church and society. When infants are baptized it is, as we have seen, in the expectation that they will be nurtured in the Christian faith and brought to the point where they will claim for themselves what has been done at their baptism. The ceremony of confirmation is designed to mark that occasion. It allows for personal confession of faith, and prayer is offered for those who have been baptized in infancy, that they may be strengthened in their discipleship. Confirmation has been called 'the sacrament of the Holy Spirit', because in most liturgies the Holy Spirit is seen as the active agent in the strengthening of discipleship. In the Catholic and Anglican traditions, confirmation has traditionally marked the point at which someone is admitted to Holy Communion on a regular basis.

In recent years confirmation has come under intense scrutiny and its value has been widely questioned. In practice confirmation has sometimes been seen as a kind of passing out parade, marking the end of a young person's association with the Christian community rather than a strengthening of their continuing discipleship. Recent theological thinking has also begun to take much more seriously the fact that baptism, at whatever age it is administered, is initiation into the Christian community and does not need to be supplemented by some subsequent rite. As we have seen, this has important implications for such issues as the admission of young children to Holy Communion. These considerations, it has been argued, render confirmation redundant. The case is a good one. Nevertheless, there is a clear need for some occasion when those baptized in infancy can make a public profession of their faith and, perhaps for this reason, confirmation persists in the practice of most churches.

2. *Penance*

The Christian church has always wrestled with the question of how those Christians who have committed sin may confess that sin, receive assurance of forgiveness and be reconciled to the church. At some stages in the church's history, sins committed after a person has been baptized have been viewed with great seriousness, requiring public penance and reconciliation. Sometimes church discipline has required that people make their act of 'confession' (as penance is popularly called) to an authorized minister of the church prior to receiving Holy Communion. Even when that has not been the case, the church has always made provision for those with troubled consciences to express their repentance and receive an appropriate assurance of forgiveness. Penance involves taking seriously the fact that our sins are not only against God, they are often also against the church community (Matthew 18.15–18). The New Testament recognizes that acknowledgment of sin and prayer for one another lies at the heart of a spiritually healthy church community (James 5.18).

3. *Marriage.*

Marriage was not instituted by the Christian church. Ceremonies in which a man and a woman give themselves to each other in a marriage relationship can be found in most societies, though what is involved in this varies widely. The New Testament records how Jesus spoke positively about marriage, viewing it as a gift of God (Mark 10.6–9) and on one occasion graced a village wedding with his presence (John 2.1–11). A number of passages in the New Testament letters give teaching about the nature of marriage between Christian people (and, indeed, where one of the partners is not a Christian). At one point, the love of a husband for his wife is compared to the love Christ has for the church (Ephesians 5.25). In the light of this it is perhaps surprising that the Christian church did not become involved in marriage ceremonies for many years and it was not until the twelfth century that theologians began to speak of it as a sacrament. Although marriage is not a Christian invention, when it began to be celebrated in church it quickly acquired some distinctively Christian features. The most important of these is that such marriage is intended to be lifelong. All Christian denominations offer marriage services, although in many societies these have to be supplementary to the legal requirements of the state.

4. *Ordination*

Ordination is the act of setting someone apart for ministry in the church of God. Jesus chose his disciples and set them apart (Mark 3.13–19; Matthew 10.1–4; Luke 6.13–16), though it would hardly be appropriate to describe this act as ordination. The New Testament records various forms of ministry within the church (I Corinthians 12.27–31; Ephesians 4.11–12) and a number of occasions on which people were commissioned for specific ministries by the laying on of hands (e.g., Acts 6.6; Acts 13.1–3). Such laying on of hands is what we now call ordination, and it is referred to several times, particularly in the Pastoral Epistles (I Timothy 4.14; 5.22). The Catholic and Orthodox traditions value what is called the 'historic succession' in which it is believed that, for an ordination to be valid, it must be possible to trace it right back to the apostles themselves. For Christians who think in this way, ordination confers a priestly character on the one who receives it. Other Christians specifically deny that a priestly character is conferred by ordination, believing this to be incompatible with the New Testament teaching about the priesthood of Christ. They would also deny the necessity for any 'historic succession', arguing that the grace of God cannot be made to depend in this kind of way on historical events. Nevertheless, most churches practise ordination by the laying on of hands, and such ordinations serve to make those who receive them ministers of the church of God, authorized to focus the priesthood of the people of God. Understandably perhaps, those who lay stress on the 'historic succession' often have real difficulties with the idea of ordaining women, because the apostles, from whom such ordinations are thought to be derived, were all men. Those churches which do not believe in the 'historic succession' are able to approach the question of the ordination of women from a different perspective.

5. *Unction*

Unction involves prayer and anointing with oil of those who are sick or dying. At one time this was known as 'extreme unction', which, as that name implies, was reserved for those who were gravely ill and especially for those on the point of death. It was partly designed to prepare the sick person for death, though an element of prayer for healing and recovery has usually been part of it. In recent years there has been some new thinking in Catholic circles about unction and its purpose and the dropping of the word 'extreme' from its title indicates in which direction that thinking has moved. James 5.14–15 is usually cited as the biblical authority for the practice, and that clearly envisages the recovery of the person who has been anointed and over whom prayer has been offered. Unction is now generally thought of as designed to strengthen the faith of the sick person so that they are better able to deal with what is happening, whether that be recovery, continuing illness or death itself. Although Protestant churches do not practise unction as a distinct ceremony, there has been a major resurgence of interest in healing services (often involving the use of oil which has been blessed) in recent years. There is very little to distinguish such services from unction as it is currently practised in the Catholic tradition.

All of these ceremonies (except Confirmation) can claim some biblical authority. As we have seen, most Protestant churches practise them all in varying degrees, though they may be called by other names. And indeed, when we practise them we expect something to happen through them. When a man and a woman marry each other, a real union takes place. When a person is ordained by the laying on of hands, spiritual authority has been conveyed. When people have confessed their sins and been told that God has forgiven them, that forgiveness is real. When we pray that someone may be confirmed and strengthened in their faith, we believe that God answers prayer. When the sick have been prayed over and anointed, we recognize that God's blessing has been imparted through what has happened. Protestant Christians would have no difficulty with the idea that all these things (and others!) can be vehicles of God's love and grace to us. In that sense they can be recognized as *sacramental*. There is certainly no reason why, if God can take bread, wine and water and use them as means to convey his presence to us, he cannot do the same with oil, rings, hands, or indeed anything else.

Why then, does the Protestant tradition, whilst valuing these things, confine its understanding of what a sacrament is to Baptism and the Eucharist? The simple answer is that these two are different because these are the only two which the church believes to have been commanded by Christ. For this reason they are sometimes called the Gospel sacraments or the New Testament sacraments. Whatever may be said about scriptural authority for any or all of the other five sacraments of the Catholic tradition, it is only Baptism and the Eucharist which can claim direct institution by the Lord himself. As we have seen, Baptism was believed to have been commanded in the Great Commission towards the end of Matthew's Gospel, and the Eucharist was instituted by Jesus at the Last Supper. It is because these two sacraments are of 'Divine institution', as the phrase has it, that they are rightly regarded as pre-eminent.

Whatever genuine blessing may come through other ceremonies which the church may from time to time devise to meet the spiritual needs of Christian people, it is in Baptism and Eucharist, through Christ's warrant, that we can have certainty that the grace of God is offered to humankind.

Further Reading

General

Baptism, Eucharist and Ministry, World Council of Churches Faith and Order Paper no. 111, WCC, Geneva 1982.

A very influential ecumenical document, to which churches made formal responses at the time. There is some blandness, inevitable in a report produced by a committee. Nevertheless, this raises crucial issues and indicates what might happen through genuine ecumenical agreement.

John Macquarrie, *A Guide to the Sacraments*, SCM Press 1997.

Deals with all seven sacraments of the Catholic tradition. Disappointingly old-fashioned and unlikely to convince those not already sharing its viewpoint, yet containing a lot of useful information.

Oliver C. Quick, *The Christian Sacraments*, Nisbet 1927.

Now dated in many respects, and somewhat heavy going, it is nevertheless worth reading for its many insights.

Baptism

Donald Bridge and David Phypers, *The Water that Divides*, IVP 1977.

Explores the controversies surrounding infant baptism, including the issue of 'rebaptism', from an evangelical point of view and with a pastoral tone.

Neil Dixon, *Troubled Waters*, Epworth Press 1979.

Discusses the case for and against infant baptism, coming down firmly in favour of it but arguing for a disciplined pastoral policy.

Michael Green, *Baptism*, Hodder and Stoughton 1978.

A remarkably good little book which argues the case for infant baptism from an evangelical perspective.

David S. M. Hamilton, *Through the Waters*, T&T Clark 1990.

Exceptionally good on the biblical imagery about baptism and its relationship to the Christian life.

Lawrence Stookey, *Baptism, Christ's Act in the Church*, Abingdon Press, Nashville, USA 1990.

A stimulating exploration of a number of the issues which trouble us, stressing the priority of divine grace.

Geoffrey Wainwright, *Christian Initiation*, Lutterworth Press 1969.

Sets baptism in the wider context of initiation, and argues for child baptism rather than infant baptism.

Eucharist

Timothy Gorringe, *The Sign of Love*, SPCK 1997.

A very worthwhile small book which deals with the impact eucharistic theology and practice should have on the life of the church and the world.

John Hadley, *Bread of the World*, Darton, Longman and Todd 1989.

An accessibly written book which explores eucharistic theology in its wider aspects.

J. P. Hickinbotham, *The Open Table*, Hodder & Stoughton 1966.

A sustained plea for the Anglican communion to admit all baptized Christians as guests at the communion table. What it asks for has now happened, but much of the material is still useful in considering intercommunion within the wider church.

Paul McPartlan, *Sacrament of Salvation*, T&T Clark 1995.

A useful book from a Roman Catholic author, looking at the way the Eucharist shapes our understanding of the church.

Kenneth Stevenson, *Accept This Offering*, SPCK 1989.

A distinguished liturgist discusses the way in which our understanding of the Eucharist as a sacrifice helps us to relate worship to life.

Max Thurian, *The Mystery of the Eucharist*, Mowbray 1983.

Translation of a French original. It discusses the doctrine of the Real Presence and attempts to find some ecumenical convergence.

Geoffrey Wainwright, *Eucharist and Eschatology*, Epworth Press 1971.

A very important book dealing with a theme there has not been space to touch on in this one, namely the way in which the Eucharist looks forward to the end of all things in Christ.

Gordon S. Wakefield, *On the Edge of Mystery*, Epworth Press 1969.

A series of reflections on six of the texts from the communion orders in the Anglican 1662 *Book of Common Prayer* and the 1936 Methodist *Book of Offices*. A treasury of devotional insight.

G. D. Yarnold, *The Bread Which We Break*, OUP 1960.

A very fine study of various aspects of the Eucharist, stressing the relationship with Christ our great High Priest. From the 'catholic' end of Anglicanism.